De-colonising the Biblical Narrative

Anne Pattel-Gray
Norman Habel
Australian First Nations

The *Decolonising the Biblical Narrative* series is a new landmark in Biblical hermeneutics. The volumes in this series are designed to employ principles for decolonising the text to expose the colonial dimensions of the text and to retrieve pre-colonial narratives that resonate with the Ancestral Narratives of First Nations peoples.

Series Editor

Anne Pattel-Gray

Norm Habel

De-colonising the Biblical Narrative Volume 1

A FIRST NATIONS De-colonising of Genesis 1–11

Aunty Anne (Anne Pattel-Gray)
&
Australian First Nations
Edited by
Uncle Norm (Norman Habel)

Adelaide
2022

Front cover image: Based on, Artist Unknown. From Bryan AL Cranstone, A corroboree ground prepared for a totemic ceremony in central Australia, 1971.

The Australian Aborigines, London: British Museum, 1973.

ISBN:
Softcover 978-1-922582-04-1
Hardcover 978-1-922582-05-8
Epub 978-1-922582-06-5
PDF 978-1-922582-07-2

Published and edited by

Making a lasting impact
An imprint of the ATF Press Publishing Group
owned by ATF (Australia) Ltd.
PO Box 234
Brompton, SA 5007
Australia
ABN 90 116 359 963
www.atfpress.com

Contents

Preface

De-colonising the Biblical Narrative
is dedicated to
all those First Nations People of Australia
who have dared
to confront the white settlers
and missionaries
with pre-colonial spirituality
and Ancestral Narratives
but were dismissed as godless pagans,
when in reality
their spiritual bond
with the Creator Spirit in the Land
is even more profound
than the spiritual bond
of many traditional Christians
with their God Almighty
high in the heavens.

Participants Introduce Themselves

I am Anne Pattel-Gray

It is important for our readers to understand the background of how this work began. It all started with discussions between Dr Norm Habel (Old Testament Scholar) and myself (an Australia First Nation's Scholar) at a national conference titled, 'Common Dreams', where we both delivered keynote addresses in 2019 in Sydney along with many others.

Norm shared his work on *'Acknowledgement of the Land and Faith of Aboriginal Custodians—after following the Abraham Trail'*, where he described his goal to follow the Abraham trail through the legends of Genesis and beyond to retrieve, where possible, how Abraham related to the Indigenous Canaanites, their God and their Land.[1] What he believed he had retrieved provides a precedent for the colonial invaders who have dispossessed the Land of Australia and discounted the faith of the First Nations they invaded. In the light of the Abraham precedent and subsequent colonial history, it is time to go beyond making another apology and make a formal acknowledgement that leads to a genuine treaty process.

I mentioned to Norm how the biblical narrative regarding Genesis belongs to the Israelites as this is their creation story. We Australia First Nations have our own creation stories that reflect the action and interaction of the Creator or Supreme Being in our worldview.

This commenced our discourse regarding Australia First Nations Creation stories and our understanding of the Creator's actions

1. Norman Habel, *Acknowledgement of the Land and Faith of Aboriginal Custodians after Following the Abraham Trail* (Melbourne: Morning Star, 2018).

and interactions through our Spirit Ancestors in the creation of our world, humanity, customs, laws, ceremonies, songs, rituals, connection to Land, water and sea, language, cosmology, worldview and philosophy—this being the basis to the formation of First Nations identity, faith and spirituality.

Australia First Nations have a deep understanding of the Creator that has been nurtured over 60,000 years and we give deep reverence to the secret/sacred Ancestral Narratives pertaining to the Creator Spirit as this holds great significance in our Spiritual world.

Identifying the Indigenous peoples in biblical narratives has contributed to and informed our discourse and the focus of the exegetical and hermeneutical process which we First Nations Australia take to explore this topic further. Especially through our collective experience, we First Nations are able to read through a First Nations lens which brings a new insight to our theology and grounds it within an Australian context.

To begin this part of our methodology we must include the process of de-colonising our minds, ideology and belief systems that have held many of us captive to a Western interpretation. We believe that the Creator Spirit was here in our beginnings long before white colonisers invaded our Land. We believe we can now find the freedom to interpret our relationship with the Spirit Creator through our worldview, as we listen with a de-colonised mind to narratives of Genesis.

I will also explore ancient Ancestral Narratives that speak of the Creator Spirit's actions and interaction with Australia First Nations by defining the Creator's relationship within our understanding and worldview before colonial invasion.

This method sets the foundation for the construction of a First Nations hermeneutical and exegetical process which allows us the freedom to re-read the biblical narratives from our own pre-colonial perspective. In doing this we are challenged to de-colonise our minds and to be open to the opportunity of reading the biblical texts through First Nations eyes and understandings.

This will enable us to examine our discourse and to consider how indoctrinated we are by Euro-centric colonial philosophy, values, and culture and unveil the forced domination of Western biblical interpretation to which First Nations have been held in bondage. This endeavour is to develop a truly Australian First Nations theology born out of and embedded in our Land—Our Mother Earth.

I am Uncle Norm

I have been listening to Australian First Nations elders for many years, constantly aware of my being part of a cruel colonial culture here in Australia. Sad to say, I was born a colonial kid surrounded by colonial worldviews in First Nations country occupied by German settlers.

I am deeply indebted to Uncle George Rosendale who helped me de-colonise the Scriptures and my mind. He returned to his ancestors in 2019. More recently, I have been challenged once again to discern First Nations dimensions of the stories in the Bible, stories that are meaningful for the First Nations people of this Land. In that context, the insights of Anne Pattel-Gray have been profound. For that reason, I have chosen, as an empathetic editor, to cooperate with Anne and other First Nations People of Australia to engage in a new venture: *De-colonising the Biblical Narrative,* beginning with a de-colonising of Genesis 1–11.

If I am to de-colonise my brain further, I need to face the fact that for most of my life I have treated the Bible texts as 'texts,' whether that be the Hebrew text, the Greek text, the King James Bible or even the Earth Bible. I must now come to terms with the reality that the Genesis narratives were not originally texts at all. They were oral legends and traditions told and retold among the peoples from before Abraham's day.

Texts in the Old Testament only became a reality as 'texts' during the exile when the Israelites chose to preserve their traditions in written format, reflecting the colonial mindset of their day.

To de-colonise my mind, therefore, I need to listen to the narrative retrieved from the text rather than focus on the written text as such. Pre-colonial narratives were originally oral traditions like the oral Ancestral Narratives of the First Nations Australia,

More than twenty years ago I worked with the Rainbow Spirit Elders of Australia to create an influential volume entitled *Rainbow Spirit Theology* (2007). The time has come for the voice of the Australian First Nations to be heard again as they listen to the biblical narrative, guided by the voice of the Spirit in the Land. Back in the 1960s, Jomo Kenyatta, an anti-colonial activist, who became prime minister of Kenya, wrote:

> *When the missionaries arrived, the Africans had the Land, and the missionaries had the Bible. They taught us how to pray with our eyes closed. When we opened them, they had the Land and we had the Bible.*[2]

The same has been said about the situation in Australia, but it need not continue to be so. The now famous *Uluru Statement from the Heart* calls for Australian leaders to acknowledge the sovereignty of the Australian First Nations, including their spiritual relationship with the Land. Many First Nations Australians are also ready to challenge the traditional 'colonial' reading and interpretation of the biblical narratives. And I, as an editor who knows the original Hebrew language of the Old Testament, am only too willing to re-read the biblical narrative and de-colonise the text with First Nations Australia.

Over the years I have employed a range of approaches to interpret the biblical text, everything from theological, historical, literary and ecological hermeneutics. I am now ready to take a radical leap and introduce a 'de-colonising hermeneutic.'

First Nation Participants

The initial contributors to this volume were the Rainbow Spirit Elders led by Uncle George Rosendale, from the *Guugu Yimithirr* nation. Uncle George was Uncle Norm's primary tutor in how to de-colonise the Bible. These First Nations Christian elders prepared the volume on *Rainbow Spirit Theology* at two weeklong workshops in 1996 and 1997.

In the Introduction to *Rainbow Spirit Theology* (1997), the Rainbow Spirit Elders express their belief that they can read the Landscape as their Scriptures and as a result have a colonial-free approach, listening to the Scriptures as they listen to the Land.

> *The Bible is also a source of theology for Christian Aboriginal people. We accept that God has spoken and continues to speak through the Christian Scriptures. This God of the Scriptures is known to Aboriginal people as the Creator Spirit,* ***who speaks to us through the Land.*** *The Land is like the Scriptures—sacred*

2. Steve Heinrichs, *Unsettling the Word. Biblical Experiments in De-colonisation*, edited by Steve Heinrichs (Canada: Mennonite Church, 2018), xvii.

> *stories and signs are inscribed in the Landscape and are readily available to those who can read them.*[3]

To discern the truth, the Rainbow Spirit Elders believe that they must first read the Landscape and listen to the Creator Spirit speaking through the Land. The word heard from the biblical Scriptures must resonate with the truth heard from the Land Scriptures, heard for many thousands of years and celebrated in the Ancestral Narrative ceremonies. According to the Rainbow Spirit Elders, *the Creator Spirit, has been* ***speaking*** *through Aboriginal culture from the beginning.*[4]

At a recent workshop focusing on the interpretation of the creation traditions of Genesis 1–11, some First Nations Australian Christians confessed that they were not only inspired by their rich Ancestral heritage and their spiritual bond with the Land, but also by the truth that Christ liberated them from the colonial sins that had enslaved their minds and that Christ had freed them to search for the truth by de-colonising the biblical narrative.

Insights from these workshop participants and interested First Nation Australians from around the country have also been included in this volume, even elders who were 'colonised' in mission stations and were taught that the Rainbow Spirit—often portrayed as a Rainbow Snake—was the Rainbow Serpent, otherwise known as Satan.

First Nations participants in the workshop in Adelaide, March 2021, were Anne Pattel-Gray, Brooke Prentis, Clyde Rigney, Rose Rigney, Denise Champion, Sean Weetra, Ken Sumner and Grant Paulson. White fellas who had de-colonised their minds and participated include Norman Habel, Ian Dempster, Howard Amery and Vicky Balabanski who dared to name colonising as 'sin'.

---

3. Rainbow Spirit Elders, *Rainbow Spirit Theology. Towards an Australian Aboriginal Theology* (Adelaide/Cambridge: ATF Press/Cambridge University Press, 2007), 20.
4. Rainbow Spirit Elders, *Rainbow Spirit Theology*, 11.

Introduction

The Colonial Context

In previous years, most non-indigenous biblical scholars in Australia, have translated, read and interpreted biblical narratives like Genesis 1–11 from a colonial perspective, even if they were not conscious of their colonial orientation.

The time has come to acknowledge that the Bible itself, from the time of the first settlers and missionaries, has been a tool of the colonising process. Steven Heinrichs writes:

> *The Bible has been used as a tool of colonialism, xenophobia, exclusion and cultural genocide. It still is. But this does not have to be. For centuries, communities of radical compassion and courage have read and re-read the sacred page in creative and critical fashion, so that these old memories shake the powers from their thrones and bring actual change to those who have been kept down.*[1]

Given the long history of reading the Bible from a colonial perspective and acknowledging that a colonial reading helped to justify the colonisation of Aboriginal peoples, the key question is whether First Nations Australians can de-colonise their minds and 're-read the sacred page' free from colonial control.

At the very time *Rainbow Spirit Theology* was being written in Australia, Michael Prior outlined how the Bible was a powerful factor in the colonial history of Latin America, South Africa and Palestine. In relation to Latin America, he writes,

1. Heinrichs, *Unsettling the Word*, xvii.

> *Richards judges that 'the problem is not the Bible itself, but the way it has been interpreted'. The task of the indigenous peoples, in such a view, is to construct a new hermeneutic which de-colonises the interpretation of the Bible and takes possession of it from an indigenous perspective.*[2]

In the light of this challenge, we—Uncle Norm, Anne Pattel-Gray and other First Peoples of Australia—have come together to explore how to interpret a book that has had a history of being a tool for colonising the Land and humiliating the First Nations peoples of the Land

Our approach in *De-colonising the Biblical Narrative* is not only to 'de-colonise ***the interpretation*** of the Bible,' but also to 'de-colonise the biblical narrative itself.'

In this context, colonialism can be understood as a mindset of editors, individuals, communities or peoples that assume, claim or activate the fundamental belief or worldview that they have the right to exercise dominion, control or dispossession of other individuals, countries, communities or peoples.

Recently, Meredith Lake published a relevant volume entitled *The Bible in Australia: A Cultural History*. In Chapter 11 she speaks about 'Indigenising the Bible', and explores the many ways in which the Bible has played a role in colonising the First Peoples of Australia. She begins by claiming that,

> *The Bible came in a European imperial guise, wrapped up in colonial thought and culture. Various interpretations of the Bible played into the ways the colonists thought about the Land they claimed and occupied.*[3]

> *By the mid-twentieth century, there was a significant tradition of Indigenous Australians drawing on the Bible in response to colonialism.*[4]

In addition to her detailed analysis of how the Bible affected the lives and cultures of the First Nations Australians and the various ways in

---

2. Michael Prior, *The Bible and Colonialism. A Moral Critique* (Sheffield: Sheffield Academic Press, 1997), 69.
3. Meredith Lake, *The Bible in Australia: A Cultural History* (Sydney: NewSouth Publishing, 2018), 46.
4. Lake, *The Bible in Australia*, 327.

which they sought to relate the Bible to their culture, Meredith Lake also makes the following claim:

> *The Bible remains deeply important for Australia today, because it is at once an embedded part of our European inheritance, and a source for subverting colonial power and reconciling the nation. It is a text that crosses and reshapes boundaries.*[5]

The challenge we face is to confront the readers and interpreters of the Bible in the churches and communities of Australia with the truth that their approach has been conditioned by generations of sermons, songs, culture and beliefs that assume that their traditional colonial way of interpreting the Bible in precisely the way God intended, without taking into account the colonial factors that conditioned their approach OR that there might be an alternative First Nations approach.

De-colonising Hermeneutics

The interpretation process in relation to the Earth Bible commentaries has been summarised as *Suspicion, Identification and Retrieval.*[6] The interpreter suspects/assumes that past interpretations of the text may have been anthropocentric, the focus being exclusively on human beings and their relationship with God. The interpreter then seeks to identify with the non-human components of the text, elements such as Earth, Land, forest, waters and the like, and to ascertain their role in the plot, thought or orientation of the text. In so doing, the empathetic interpreter may seek to retrieve the latent voice or message of these non-human elements.

Similar steps will be involved in the hermeneutical process of de-colonising biblical narratives, namely,

- Suspicion
- Exposure
- Retrieval
- Response.

---

5. Lake, *The Bible in Australia*, 8.
6. Norman Habel & Peter Trudinger, *Exploring Ecological Hermeneutics* (Atlanta: Society of Biblical Literature, 2008), 1–8.

These steps are similar but not identical with those employed in the Earth Bible series noted above. The orientation in this new hermeneutic is the colonial worldview not an anthropocentric worldview. The goal of the Earth Bible hermeneutics was to retrieve the voice/perspective of the non-human components of the narrative. The goal of the de-colonising hermeneutic is to retrieve the pre-colonial narrative or tradition.

Suspicion

The interpreter—one of the First Nations Christians of Australia, or an empathetic reader with a de-colonised mind, who dares to identify with the worldview of First Nation Australian—will be ready to suspect three colonial factors in previous readings of the narrative.

1. The Language

The reader may discover that the translation of the text in recent generations reflects a colonial orientation rather than the orientation of the original story in the tradition. This is immediately obvious in the very first verse of the Bible, where we discover colonial translations such as,

> *In the beginning God created the heavens and the Earth and the Earth was . . .*

The original Hebrew in this verse does not refer to the celestial realm called the heavens as the abode of a deity or to the domain we call planet Earth, a cosmology that is part of a later colonial worldview.

The original Hebrew reference in Genesis 1.1 is to 'sky' and 'Land', not to heaven and Earth. The ancient listener can relate to the visible world of sky and Land where the narrative is being told. The First Nations listener of Australia is delighted to be able to do the same if we translate,

> *When God began to transform the sky and the Land, the Land was . . . .*

To discern the colonial colour of a particular word, expression or idiom in the translation, the reader may need to return to the Hebrew or Greek original to ascertain whether the translation reflects a colonial mindset for the listener. Where a translator is not a member of a First Nations community as such, he or she will need to try and de-colonise the mind and listen empathetically to the voice of First Nations colleagues in the listening process.

2. The Interpreter

Virtually all the classic interpretations of the Bible in Australia, whether by academics, clergy or missionaries, reflect the colonial mindset of the interpreter. Until recently, relatively few First Nations Australians have been involved in interpreting the original oral narrative publicly in the light of their traditional Australian culture. In many contexts, the First Nations Australians have been unduly influenced by early missionaries who reflected the colonial culture of the early settlers and, in some cases, claim to have brought God to the Land of Australia.

A First Nations approach, therefore, requires the listener to ignore traditional interpretations and to start from scratch, listening with a de-colonised mindset, to discern the language, content and intent of the original narrative tradition, in and of itself.

3. The Narrator

An interpretation factor that has rarely been considered is the potential colonial orientation of the narrator or editor of the biblical text itself. Despite the conservative tradition that biblical authors were inspired by God, they were in fact interpreters of their time who gathered oral traditions from the past and transformed them into relevant narratives or poems that often reflect the colonial orientation of the Israelite peoples from the days of Moses to their return from exile in Babylon.

Listening with a de-colonised mind, we can raise again the possibility that the writers/narrators/editors of the tradition were also writing from an ancient colonial perspective that was part of their world, even if the context was very different from the colonial orientation of Western peoples of today.

Exposure

The goal of a de-colonising hermeneutic is not only to become aware of past colonial translations and interpretations of the narrative, but also to focus on the specific colonial dimensions of the narrative, be they reflected in the language, the idioms, the content or the theology of the narrative.

This process also involves developing a 'colonial consciousness' that facilitates discerning those traditions that reflect a colonial orientation, however subtle that may be. The *imago Dei* text in Genesis 1.26–28, for example, is replete with the colonial language of dominion and subjugation. According to the written text of most translations, humans are created to reflect God's celestial power, having 'dominion' over living creatures and a mandate to 'subdue/ colonise' the Land.

De-colonising the narrative involves daring to identify the unrecognised curse of colonialism that has led translators and interpreters to justify colonialism as a divine right in ancient and modern societies. Our goal is to expose that 'colonial curse' within the text and acknowledge its impact in classic interpretations.

Retrieval

The process of identifying the colonial dimensions of the narrative also enables the interpreter to retrieve narratives that do not reflect a colonial bias, but which resonate with one or more truths or Ancestral Narratives of the First Nations Australians of today.

As an aside, we need to indicate that we use the designation 'Ancestral Narrative,' both for the colonial-free narratives retrieved from the biblical text and for the narratives of First Nations Australia that were once designated 'Dreaming Stories/Narratives'.

When we hear the blessing of Melchizedek, the Canaanite Priest of Salem, for example, we can immediately recognise an Ancestral Narrative that has survived later editing by colonial narrators. The original indigenous Canaanite blessing formula preserved in Genesis 14.19 reads,

> *Blessed be Abram by El Elyon,*
> *Maker of sky and Land.*

This blessing is clearly a Canaanite blessing, not a later Israelite blessing. Not only is the priest a Canaanite, but the God involved is El, the Canaanite Creator Spirit associated with the Land of Canaan.

The First Nations listener, moreover, may not only identify the blessing as free from colonial editing, but also may feel inclined to identify with Abraham or Melchizedek and receive a blessing from El, the Canaanite Creator Spirit who is one with the Creator Spirit of the Land in Australia.

In some contexts, our task will not only be to retrieve ancient texts that are free from colonial additions, but also to take the bold imaginative step of de-colonising narratives that are blatantly colonial. This is especially crucial, for example, in discerning the original Wisdom tradition embedded in the Fall Narrative of Genesis 3.

A knowledge of the original Hebrew of Greek is also crucial to retrieve the original words, idioms or expressions that have been clouded by the colonial narrator or interpreter.

Response

To demonstrate the relevance of de-colonising the original narrative and retrieving narratives free from colonial bias, we have invited fellow First Nations Australian listeners to respond, describing their resonance with the text as a narrative that is in harmony with the Ancestral Narratives of their Country.

Some colonial-oriented texts, however, may also prove offensive and abusive to the First Nation listener, especially if God is portrayed as involved in the colonial bias of the text. It is especially abusive, for example, when First Nations Australians hear the story of Joshua as a positive reading of the book of Joshua by Australians who portray Joshua as a divinely endorsed precedent for the invasion and settlement of Australia as the Promised Land.

Narratives that are free from colonial editing, however—such as the commissioning of the first human being to 'serve' and 'preserve' the Land in Eden (Gen 2.25)—resonate with First Nations listeners who believe they are commissioned to be custodians of the Land in Australia and beyond. The process of listening to the subtleties and nuances of the narrative is vital for listeners, whether they be First Nations Australians or empathetic Christians who have de-colonised their minds to hear the voice of the ancient storytellers.

The Colonial Curse

In the initial workshop exploring our de-colonising approach, one of the participants spoke of the 'colonial curse,' an expression that may seem rather excessive to some but was understood to be valid by the First Nations people present. The term encapsulates the extensive acts of abuse, slaughter and vilification of First Nations Australia by many of the early colonial settlers. Some early leaders even spoke of 'Aboriginal Canaanites' being the lowest form of humanity.

Significantly, however, we can return to the colonial biblical traditions to discern just such a curse. As we will discover in our interpretation of Genesis 9, Canaan is cursed by Noah, and his descendants are destined to be slaves for his brothers. Workshop participants testified that they had been identified as descendants of this curse: the curse of Ham.

In Joshua 6, when the Israelites are about to conquer the Canaanite city of Jericho, Joshua declares that the city is to be cursed—or in the ruthless language of the original, 'devoted to the colonial God, YHWH, by exterminating it' (Jos 6:17).

The colonial process—from the initial colonisation of Canaan to the contemporary colonisation of Australia—has been replete with cruel actions that validly described as colonial curses.

The Challenge

The challenge before us is to move beyond traditional colonial approaches to interpreting the biblical text and dare to de-colonise the narrative to retrieve an ancient narrative that is not only free from colonial bias but resonates with the spirit of the Ancestral Narratives of First Nations Australia.

Chapter One
The Primal Land Narrative:
Land Is Born, Comes to Life and Creates Life

The first Narrative
in the Bible,
heard by an audience,
prior to colonial control,
is not a myth about the origins
of Heaven and Earth,
but an Ancestral Narrative
about the primordial Deep
being transformed,
enabling Land to be born,
come to life
and become the mother
of all Land beings.

The Ancestral Land Narrative of Genesis 1:1–25, 29–31, 2:1–3

The Land in the Deep (vv 1–2)

*When God began to **transform** the Sky and the Land, **the Land** was a **formless mass** and darkness was on the face of the **Deep**. **And the Wind** of God hovered over the face of the waters.*

The Light and Darkness (vv 3–5)

*Then God said, 'Let there be **light**. And there was light. And God saw the light that it was good. And God set the light apart from the darkness. God called the light 'Day', and the darkness he called 'Night'.*

The Division of the Waters (vv 6–8)

Then God said, 'Let there be a ***canopy in*** *the waters and let it divide the waters from the waters.' So, God made a canopy and it divided the waters under it from the waters above it. And it happened! And God named the* ***canopy, 'Sky'.***

The Land Is Born (vv 9–10)

Then God said, 'Let the waters below the Sky come together into one place and let the ground ***appear.'*** *And it happened! God named the ground* ***'Land'*** *and the waters that came together he named* ***'Seas'.*** *And God saw that it was good.*

The Land Comes Alive (vv 11–13)

Then God said, 'Let ***Land come alive*** *with vegetation, plants yielding seed and trees bearing fruit in which there is seed, according to its kind, upon the Land'. And it happened!*

The Land came alive *with vegetation, plants yielding seed according to their kind and trees bearing fruit in which there is seed according to their kind. And God saw that it was good.*

Lights for The Land (vv 14–19)

Then God said, 'Let there be lights in the canopy of the Sky to divide the day from the night; and let them be for ***signs and for seasons****, for days and for years. And let there be lights in the ceiling of the sky to give* ***light to the Land.*** *And it happened.*

Then God made two great lights, the greater light to rule the day and the lesser light to rule the night; he also made the stars. God placed the lights in the Sky to ***give light to the Land*** *to rule over the Day and the Night and divide the light from the darkness. And God saw that it was good.*

The Waters Come Alive (vv 20–23)

Then God said, 'Let ***the waters come alive*** *with swarms of life and let birds fly above the Land across the canopy of the Sky'. So God made great sea monsters and every creature that lives in the waters to reproduce and to fill the Sea, according to its kind and every winged bird according its kind. And God saw that it was good.*

*Then God blessed them and said, 'Be fruitful and multiply and fill the waters of the Seas and let birds multiply on **the Land**.'*

The Land Creates Life (vv 24–25, 29–31)

*Then God said, 'Let **the Land bring forth life**, each according to its kind: animals, creeping creatures and Land life according to its kind.' And it happened. So, God made **the life of the Land**, each according to its kind, animals and creeping creatures according to their kind.' And God saw that it was good.*

*Then God said, 'Behold I have given you every plant yielding seed which is upon **the face of the Land**, and every tree with seed in its fruit; you shall have them for food. And to every animal of the Land, and to every bird of the Sky, and to everything that creeps on the Land, everything that has the breath of life, I have given every green plant for food.' And it happened. God saw everything that he had made, and behold it was very good.*

Rest for the Land (2:1–4a)

***The Sky and the Land** were completed and all their living host. And when God completed the work which he had done, he rested. So, God blessed the day he rested and made it sacred, because on it God rested from all his creative work.*

These are the origins of the Sky and the Land
when they were transformed!

Analysis

A Preserved Ancient Tradition

The claim that we have been able to retrieve an ancient Ancestral Narrative from within the text of Genesis 1 may be considered untenable and even foolish by some European interpreters. After all, renowned scholars such as Gerhard von Rad insisted that Genesis 1 is a carefully constructed unity. He argues:

> *What is said here is intended to be true entirely and exactly as it stands. There is no trace of the hymnic element in the language,*

> *nor is there anything that is said that needs to be understood symbolically or whose deeper meaning has to be deciphered.*[1]

In spite of von Rad's famous claim that this chapter is a carefully constructed chapter with a unified theological perspective of an Israelite writer in the so-called Priestly tradition, we are bold enough to maintain that this chapter, like many others in Genesis, preserves an ancient tradition that is free from colonial influence—or in the Australian context, an oral First Nations' Ancestral Narrative—and that a later colonial narrator has preserved an earlier oral tradition, with minimal additions, in the overall narrative of Genesis.

Key Hebrew Terms

bara'— frequently translated 'create'. In view of the rendering of *'erets*, 'Land,' as being *tohu wabohu,* usually rendered 'without form', it is logical to render *bara'* as ***'transform',*** an expression used by the Rainbow Spirit Elders.[2]

'erets —often translated as 'Earth'. The basic meaning, however, is ***'Land'*** as in the expression 'Land of Canaan'. The translation 'Earth' suggests, in the mind of modern readers, 'planet Earth'.

shamayim—often translated 'heavens'. It is clear from the second stage of the transformation process that the reference is to the canopy formed to divide the waters— namely, ***the sky***— not the celestial domain of the gods.

ruach—is the everyday word for 'wind' in the Hebrew language but may also be rendered 'spirit'.

ra'ah—is a common word meaning 'be seen' or 'appear'. In some contexts, it implies revelation as when God 'appears'.

The Primordial Deep

The first two verses of this narrative are not a 'Preamble' declaring God to be the Creator of all things *ex nihilo*, 'out of nothing'. Rather, it

1. Gerhard von Rad, *Genesis. A Commentary* (London: SCM Press, 1972), 47.
2. Rainbow Spirit Elders, *Rainbow Spirit Theology*, 76.

is a portrayal of the pre-existing primordial world, named the Deep. Nor is the Deep another name for a primordial turbulent chaos as some scholars have suggested.

The Deep is a pre-existing world awaiting the transforming power of the hovering Creator Spirit.

The Deep consists of darkness, deep waters and a formless mass beneath the waters. Above the waters hovers the Wind or Spirit of God. In the several stages that follow, the primordial Deep is transformed from darkness into darkness and light, from one mass of waters into two realms of waters divided by the Sky, and from a formless mass below the waters into a vibrant visible entity that 'appears' above the waters. This entity is named 'Land,' comes alive and gives birth to living beings.

The waters below the Sky are transformed into an ocean of living sea creatures. The Sky is transformed into a realm filled with lights that provide signs, directions, seasons and light for the Land.

No Heaven and Earth

The very first verses refer to God transforming the *shamayim* and the *'erets*. These two words have regularly been translated as 'Heaven' and 'Earth'. This translation, however, reflects the cosmology of a later colonial world in which 'heaven' represents a celestial realm and Earth represents a realm below heaven, or in more recent times 'planet Earth'.

A close listening to the original text, however, reveals that *shamayim* refers to the' Sky'. The Sky was the canopy formed in stage two of the transformation process, not the 'heavens' where an Almighty God was believed to reside, according to some colonial traditions. The *shemayim* is the Sky, a canopy that divides the waters above from the waters below.

The ancient listener would have understood the everyday word *'erets*, as the normal Hebrew term for 'Land,' not planet Earth, a phenomenon unknown in the ancient world. This *'erets,* moreover, pre-exists like an embryo in the waters of the great Deep—a primordial reality widely accepted in the ancient Near East and an image that is appreciated by First Nations Australia.

In the third stage of the transforming process, God does not say, 'Let there be Earth/Land' but 'Let the waters come together and let the ground appear'. The waters burst and Land is 'born'. God names the embryo that emerges 'Land'.

Land is the name for the featureless mass that rises from the waters of the primordial Deep. Land is an emergence from the Deep below, not a creation by the word of a celestial being above. In this narrative, Land is the primary realm that emerges and comes to life. Land is not created out of nothing but is born of the primordial Deep.

The Land

Land—from the very first lines in this Ancestral Narrative to the closing word from God—is the pivotal component, the central theme, of this chapter and many subsequent chapters. This narrative is not about the origins of the universe, as some understand it today; relates the story of the Land from its primordial presence like an embryo in the Deep, to its emergence from the waters of the Deep, and to its role as the source of life for everything from plants to wild animals.

According to Deborah Bird Rose, in Aboriginal traditions of Central Australia, the primordial scene is not all that different. The dominant image is that of an unproductive and empty desert awaiting the emergence of life.[3]

When storytellers recounted this part of the narrative, they would not only have emphasised the birth of Land as a future source of life, but also the expression 'appear'. This term is frequently used to refer to a divine appearance or revelation of God (e.g., Genesis 18.2). The 'appearance' of Land is a pivotal spiritual moment in the Ancestral Narrative to which the listener would have been aware. Land is both born and revealed!

The function of the sun and moon in the sky is to provide seasons and signs for the Land. The Land persists as the centre of divine attention in this narrative of Genesis 1. God places the lights in the sky to give 'light to the Land'.

The life-giving forces in the Land become apparent when the Land comes alive and gives birth to vegetation, animal life and creatures that crawl or fly. Land is indeed Mother Earth or—preferably—Mother Land or even Co-creator Land. Land for First Nations people is seen as the life source for all living eco-systems, creatures and human beings. Land provides shelter, food, water, medicine, spiritual significance and connection to Land. Connection to Land is the source of identity, tribal belonging, inclusion, culture and law.

3. Deborah Bird Rose, *Dingo Makes Us Human. Life and Land in Australian Aboriginal Culture* (Cambridge: Cambridge University Press, 1992), 42.

The Wind

It is important to recognise that God is not depicted as a powerful celestial being who intervenes from on high to create a universe *ex nihilo*.

In the opening scene of the narrative, the listener would have heard the word *ruach*, which is the everyday Hebrew word for 'wind' (for example, Gen 8:1). God is portrayed as the primordial 'wind' that blows across the waters of the Deep. It is understandable that this term is later translated 'Spirit'; in the context of the primordial elements of Land, waters and darkness, 'wind' is probably the meaning that the ancient listener would have understood.

The primary function of this divine Wind is to transform the domains of the primordial world:

1. to transform darkness into Light (day) and Darkness (night)
2. to divide the waters above from the waters below with the creation of the Sky
3. to burst open the waters below for the Land to appear
4. to transform the Land and the Seas into realms full of life.

When Australia First Nations people speak of the Creator's Spirit or Breath that they experience as the wind or air, it is identified as the life source of the Supreme Being—the Creator Spirit. It is this Spirit that gives life, meaning and significance to First Nations people.

No Calendar

As with First Nations people of Australia, ancient cultures, like those relating the primordial narrative of Genesis 1, did not necessarily live or operate according to the calendar of later generations. While the light in the Sky may have provided signs, directions and seasons for the community, this does not also mean a corresponding calendar of days, months and years existed.

A colonial editor seems to have turned the various stages of the process of the primordial deep being transformed into six days of creation and one day of rest, to correspond to a week in his calendar. Consistent with our de-colonising process, therefore, we have deleted the seven days inserted by the colonial editor.

The Rest Blessing

When the primordial Deep is transformed into the known world, the hovering Creator Spirit rests. Resting is the final stage in the process of transforming the Land and is identified as special time to receive blessing. Rest, it would seem, is an integral part of the design of this primordial world—a nurturing dimension that benefits all creatures and all domains, including The Land.

The act of blessing involves imparting life, energy and the spiritual, an act that transforms the rest process into a life-giving dimension in the design of the primordial world, a dimension typical of the Ancestral period in the culture of the First Nations of Australia.

Voice of the First Nations

The Voice of The Rainbow Spirit Elders

The Rainbow Spirit Elders maintain that 'Rainbow Spirit Theology assumes that God, the Creator Spirit has been speaking through Aboriginal culture from the beginning'.[4] In an appendix to their book *Rainbow Spirit Theology*, the elders declare:

> *The image of the Land as a given (Gen 1:2), waiting to be* ***transformed*** *into Land and sky as we know them, is also typical of the picture of 'Land at the beginning' in Aboriginal Dreaming stories . . . The imagery of verse 2 makes excellent sense as Land covered with water, waiting for the Creator Spirit, in whatever form, to commence* ***transforming the scene*** *. . .. The picture is not one of a deity descending, in spectacular fashion, from some heavenly abode, to create a world out of nothing. Rather, the Creator Spirit is portrayed as a wind moving across, and closely linked with, the Land from the beginning.*[5]

> *The verb 'appear' in Genesis 1:9 is especially important here. The form of this verb is used elsewhere when God or an angel is revealed or 'appears'. The image is of the hidden Land below 'appearing'. The Land is thus a revelation, a manifestation that appears at the summons of God.*[6]

4. Rainbow Spirit Elders, *Rainbow Spirit Theology*, 11.
5. Rainbow Spirit Elders, *Rainbow Spirit Theology*, 76–77.
6. Rainbow Spirit Elders, *Rainbow Spirit Theology*, 77

> The Kimberley version of the Land as the primordial domain—the formless mass (*tohu wanohu)* of Genesis 1.1–2—is recorded in a work called *Yorro Yorro.*
>
> *Inside the Earth/Land lives—today and always—Wunggud, a big snake. She IS the Earth/Land and the primeval substance from which everything in nature is formed. She is female/njindi, 'her'.*
>
> *Before creation, she is tightly coiled into a ball of jelly-like substance, ngallalla, ywarun, 'everything soft like Jelly'.*
>
> *Wunggud is the Earth Snake, the name, body, substance and power of the Earth/Land. All of nature grows out of the body of the snake.*[7]

The full creation story of the Kimberleys is recorded in Chapter 23 of *Yorro Yorro* (Mowaljarlai, 1993).

The Voice of Galarrwuy Yunupingu

Land is not only a central reality in the lives and faith of First Nations Australia. Land is ultimately the locus of the Spirit and spirituality. As Galarrwuy Yunupingu writes,

> *Our relationship with the Land is much closer spiritually, physically, mentally than any other relationship I know of. People often ask me why Land is so vital to Aboriginal People and how it has remained so, despite the invasion of our Land and our traditions over the last two centuries. Land gives us value, and our spirituality is in the Land. The goodness that is in the Land—in the trees, in the water, in the rocks, in the beauty of the Landscape and nature— enables us to breathe, live and enjoy.*[8]

---

7. David Mowarlarjai & Jutta Malnic, *Yorro Yorro. Aboriginal Creation and the Renewal of Nature* (Rochester, Vermont: Inner Tradition, 1993), 132.
8. Galarrwuy Yunupingu, 'Concepts of Land and Spirituality', in *Aboriginal Spirituality: Past, Present, Future*, edited by Anne Pattel-Gray (Victoria: HarperCollins, 1996), 7.

The Voice of Denise Champion

In her book entitled *Anaditj*, Denise Champion reflects on how she was taught to read Genesis 1, but then discovered a new way.

> *I've come to read the scriptures in a new way. I had only read the Scriptures going immediately to 'God said let there be light'. But the other is very important: 'Darkness, formless and void'. There's something in the notion of light and darkness being equal partners.*[9]
>
> *Born again Christians lived in the light. They were children of the light. Anything associated with light was the accepted norm but anything you did in the dark was bad. Black people were not the accepted norm.*[10]

In the same context, Denise outlines an Adnyamathanha reading of Genesis 1:1–2.

In the beginning when Arrawatanha created the sky and the Land, there was no flat Land even. Arrawatanha spoke on the face of the waters, the wind was talking. The breath of Arrawatanha was speaking.[11]

Identification

I am Land.
I waited silently in the womb
the waters of the primal Deep
while the Creator Spirit
hovered overhead.

Then one day the waters burst
and I appeared above the waters,
alive and excited
as the Spirit game me a name,
'Land'!

9. Denise Champion, *Anaditj* (Adelaide: Openbook Howden, 2021), 8.
10. Champion, *Anaditj*, 8.
11. Champion, *Anaditj*, 8.

I was then animated by the Spirit
and I gave birth to
all kinds of living plants,
animals, birds and insects.

The waters around me
also gave birth
to fish, corrals. crabs
and even whales.

In the Sky above me,
the Spirit inserted bright lights
for Life to flourish
within me.

Yes, I am Land,
filled with the Spirit
and very much alive,
with all forms of Life.

Chapter Two
The *Imago Dei* Tradition

The conclusion of the first narrative
in Genesis
is an overt colonially oriented addition
to the Ancestral Narrative
of the Land coming to life,
an addition that has a different God
who creates humans
to have domination over the Land.
If we dare to de-colonise
the text of Genesis 1:26–28, however,
and retrieve a version
consistent with the Land Narrative
in Genesis 1,
the imago Dei *may well be identified as*
an imago terrae.

1. *The Colonial* imago Dei *Version of Genesis 1:26–28*

The Mandate to Dominate the Land

Then God said, 'Let us make humankind in our image, according to our likeness, and ***let them have dominion*** *over the fish of the sea, over the birds of the sky, over domestic animals, over the Land and over everything that creeps on the Land'.*

So, God formed human beings in his image, in the image of God he formed them, male and female he formed them.

Then God blessed them and God said to them, 'Be fruitful and multiply ***and fill the Land and subdue it, and have dominion*** *over the fish of the Sea and over the birds of the Sky and over every living creature that creeps on the Land'.*

Analysis

Key Hebrew Terms

Tselem—may refer to the 'likeness' of something or to a graven 'image'.

'adam—here rendered 'humankind'; in the next Genesis narrative it may be rendered 'ground being', a meaning derived from ***'adamah***, 'the ground' (Gen 2:7).

Radah—means 'rule' or 'have dominion over', like the kings and emperors of the ancient world.

Kabash—means 'crush' or subdue' often in a brutal way. It can also mean 'rape'.

The Celestial Decision

A logical conclusion to the sequence of events in verses 1–25 would be for human beings to emerge from the Land like other forms of life. Instead, in verse 26, the whole orientation of the narrative changes to what is typical of a colonial or imperial perspective. Instead of discerning a Wind or a Creator Spirit that hovers over the primal waters and separates the domains of the primordial world, we meet a celestial deity who consults with 'us', with the heavenly council, and decides to make humans in the image of the gods or celestial beings above.

A celestial decision is made to decide the fate of all things living and the Land itself. That decision is tantamount to a colonial edict.

Rule Over the Living

The image of God depicted here is one of a being with celestial power and dominion. Humans are not expected to reflect some personal or visual image of their Creator. Humans are to reflect the dominion of their Maker by having 'dominion' over everything that lives on the Land—and over the Land itself.

The verb *radah* (to rule) refers to the dominion of a king over his people. This term, *radah,* describes what kings and colonial taskmasters do (1 Kgs 4:24; 5:16) and what humans are now authorised to do: to rule over the animal kingdom.

In traditional First Nations Australia culture there is a kinship between all living beings. There is also the experience of moiety relationships in which each human, in a given tribe, has a spiritual kinship with member of the animal kingdom. This kinship with animals is one that requires First Nations people to fulfill certain obligations and responsibilities to their particular animal to ensure its longevity. Australia First Nations people ensure the animal world is respected, protected and celebrated as kin; it is not to be ruled by colonial humans.

Dominion Over the Land

The verb *kabash*, usually rendered 'subdue', is a harsh term that may also refer to crushing under foot (Micah 7:19) or the act of raping a woman (for example, Est 7:9; Neh 5:5). We could even translate this as 'rape the Land'—a blatantly imperial expression of the situation that has been used in relation to the colonisation of Australia.[1]

In brief, God commissions humans to 'colonise' the Land and overpower all creatures born of the Land in a brutal and forceful way. Moreover, if this act of 'colonising the Land' is equated with the image of God, then the God of this commission is tantamount to a tough Colonial Landlord.

As we demonstrate later, the *imago Dei* myth is not only 'qualified' in subsequent narratives—as in the Tower of Babel text—but also negated and transformed. The problem remains, however, that because of this text, the *imago Dei* tradition has become the basis for a formidable Christian doctrine and the justification of colonial domination. Our task is to discern, within Genesis 1–11, those texts that support the *imago Dei* colonial tradition, identify those texts that oppose the tradition and find ways of retrieving a colonial-free version of that tradition.

Dominion over Australia

It is important to recognise, from the outset, that this *imago Dei* text has been pivotal in justifying colonisation, as Harrison states:

---

1. Norman Habel, *An Inconvenient Text* (Adelaide: ATF Press, 2009).

> *The Bible played a pivotal role in justifications of colonisation in seventeenth century England. A number of different texts were used in these discussions, but the command to 'subdue the Earth' seems to take a central place in justifications for colonisation.*[2]

What was true of seventeenth century England persisted into the eighteenth and nineteen centuries in Lands like Australia. Early settlers viewed Australia as a wild world that needed to be tamed and subdued, dismissing the custodianship of the First Nations people of Australia.

Voice of the First Nations

As First Nations Australians we could not tolerate bearing the image of this God, nor could we find comfort in, or communion with, a God that acted like a Colonial Landlord. Is it possible, by returning to the images of God prevalent in the culture of the First Nations of Australia, to de-colonise this colonial God as we de-colonise the narratives of Genesis?

The colonial reading of Genesis sees God instructing humans to 'subdue and have dominion over' the natural world and to bend the Land and creatures to their will, and to multiply and fill the Land with their offspring.

First Nations people cannot help but contemplate that this colonial God is a distant ruler who has handed over to the human coloniser the whole created order as a resource under their oversight and for their own use and benefit. God is a faraway king who has ceded control of all the animals and plants to his human servants. This God instructs his human assistants to rule over what has been entrusted to them. If God, the heavenly monarch, has handed the whole created order over to the human colonists as his Landlords, the outcome is that they, in turn, are free to do what they want with it.

This was further seen in Western Christian interpretation that they were the 'Chosen Ones'. This reading paved the way for colonisers' early attacks on the First Nations people's religious and spiritual beliefs that the sacred spirit permeates all of nature. Western Christianity effectively sacralised the exploitation of nature by putting forward the

2. Peter Harrison, '"Fill the Earth and Subdue It": Biblical Warrants for Colonisation in Seventeenth Century England', in *Journal of Biblical History*, 29/1 (2005): 23.

concept of God as a disembodied deity uninterested in earthly affairs, which stripped the world of any spiritual significance or meaning. This created a separation between our kinship with our environment.

We First Nations Australia people firmly believe we are inextricably bound to our environment and that the Creator Spirit bestowed on us our Land and the laws, ceremony, songs, language, culture that define and determine our relationship with our world, and the obligations and responsibilities we have to care for the Land, all living creatures and our entire environment.

It is important that we realise it is essential to de-colonise Genesis—we need to restore our relationship first with the Creator Spirit and next to make a radical transformation that sees us reconnecting physically and spiritually with the Land and our common kinship with each other and all creation. We need to understand our human necessity to see ourselves as part of nature but not as nature itself, or as a power over nature. We must regard ourselves as living in nature and nature being important to our very existence. We long for our primordial sense of belonging to Mother Earth: our existence is dependent on her.

2. The *Imago Terrae*—a De-colonised Version of of Genesis 1:26–28

A retrieved de-colonised version of
the imago Dei *tradition*
would involve the Land as a co-creator
and humans in the imago terrae,
expressions of the imago Dei
at peace with their kin,
their fellow Land beings,
and with the Land
from which they were
born
and whose spirit they share.

Created in the Image of the Land

Then the Wind, the Creator Spirit, said to the Land, 'You have brought forth many Land beings. Let us now together make human beings in our image, male and female, and let their

> *nature reflect both Land and Spirit; and let them be at peace with their kindred Land beings and let them be custodians of the Land.' And it happened. Then the Wind blessed the human Land beings and said, 'It is very good'.*

Analysis

The De-colonising Task

The preceding de-colonised version of Genesis 1:26–28 is not an arbitrary translation, but an effort to retrieve the original *imago Dei* narrative in this chapter of Genesis—a retrieval that may well be designated *imago terrae*, 'image of the Land'.

The grounds for this rendering lie first, in discerning a theological and spiritual consistency with the preceding narrative (Gen 1:1–25); second, in recognising the implications of the Ancestral Narrative of Genesis 2, which is free from colonial domination.

The Spirit and the Land

In Genesis 1, verse 2, the Wind or Sprit is the creative divine Presence involved in the process of transforming the primordial world into a cosmos with Land at the centre. The dominating celestial deity of Genesis 1:26–28, however, negates the essential creative process of the hovering Wind or Spirit who is identified as the God involved in the transforming process.

The primordial Land is the source of all living things in the Ancestral Narrative of Genesis 1:1–25, an ancient narrative that precedes the *imago Dei* text. All vegetation and all species of animal life emerge from the Land. Land is therefore the logical source of human life as well. Land is the obvious co-creator of humankind.

Humans in Genesis 2

In Genesis 2, it is revealed that human beings did emerge from the 'ground' of the Land. They are 'ground beings' or 'Land beings.'

Moreover, they are not commissioned to dominate living creatures and subdue the Land but are commissioned 'to serve and preserve' the Land in Eden (Gen 2:15). The Hebrew terms for 'serve' (*'abad*) and 'preserve' (*shamar*) are diametric opposites of 'rule' and 'subdue'.

An *imago terrae* Ancestral Narrative consistent with the text of Genesis 2, therefore, is for humans to be Land beings, at one with the Land, 'at peace with their kin', 'born of the Land', and 'custodians of the Land', with whom they bear the image of the Creator Spirit present in the Land, rather than as a celestial overlord.

Voice of the First Nations

The Voice of Auntie Anne

Australia's First Nations faith has been nurtured over thousands of years and as a result we have a very intimate relationship with the Creator Spirit and when we speak of this relationship, we invoke the Spirit Creator in our midst. Our Ancestral Narratives reflect this relationship, and our ceremonies give praise to our Creator and remind us of our obligations to one another, to Land and the environment, to law and the responsibilities given to us by the Creator Spirit. Among First Nations there are power-filled stories about the Creator's acts in the very beginning. George Rosendale states in *Rainbow Spirit Theology*:

> *In the very beginning, the earth was formless and empty of life. The Creator Spirit, in the form of the Rainbow Spirit, shaped the land, its mountains, seas, rivers and trees.*[3]

Some of these stories depict the Earth as a vast featureless plain or desert until the Rainbow Spirit transforms it into the Land we know today.

Australian First Nations Christian leaders tell of their Ancestral Narratives that spoke about our knowledge and belief of a Creator who through our Spirit Ancestors formed our world and forged our identity, culture, and Law. This process highlighted the relationship between First Nations peoples, the environment, the spiritual world of our Spirit Ancestors and the Creator Spirit, and how they were all linked to each other and dependent upon this interconnection. Faith and the spiritual world for First Nations Australia were, and still are, the life force and foundation of our life, existence and survival. The Creator is the source of *life* for us and we cannot survive without our connection to the life source as stated by our Spiritual leaders.

---

3. Rainbow Spirit Elders, *Rainbow Spirit Theology*, 29.

Djankawu—Great Ancestral Spirit

Reverend Djiniyini Gondarra relates,

> *Now let me share with you a story of a Great Ancestral Spirit who is both father-mother figure of the East Arnhem Land people—from whom I am descended—called Djankawu. This Great Ancestral Spirit-figure once lived in the flesh. My people described him/her as sharing life in common with our people in the Dreamtimes. Djankawu shared with them the sacred knowledge of ceremonies, songs, dances, and the sacred stories about how things began to form in the universe and on the earth. Djankawu gave the tribes names and the kinship system, and Djankawu taught them many things such as how to use artefacts, tools and weapons to hunt for animals and to fight enemies. Djankawu was regarded as a holy sacred Being.*
>
> *Djankawu revealed himself to the men as one of them; to the women she revealed herself as a mother figure. Djankawu was seen as a divine person but, at the same time, Djankawu communicated as a human. Djankawu taught our people how to live a life of harmony and humanity. Djankawu taught our people that all living creatures are their friends and that they must care for them. Djankawu gave our people special knowledge to communicate to these creatures. Djankawu gave the tribes sacred sites ownership to each individual clan groups. Djankawu taught the tribes how to look after the Land and the seas. Djankawu taught them about the holy living and their relationship to the Mother earth.*
>
> *Djankawu kingdom is known as the 'kingdom of sunrise'; as the East Arnhem Land people say, 'We are the people of the sunrise'. When Djankawu, the Great Spirit, finished his/her work within Eastern Arnhem Land he/she took a long journey to the West to continue singing the sacred songs, to continue naming different places, plants, trees, animals and people of different clan groups, and to continue giving people sacred sites stores, ceremonies and sacred sites. This is one story of the Great Ancestral figure. There are many stories of such Great Spirit Beings right across Australia amongst our people.*[4]

4. Anne Pattel-Gray, *Aboriginal Spirituality: Past, Present, Future* (Melbourne: HarperCollins Religious, 1996), 44–45.

Identification

I am Land.
I not only gave birth
to all kinds of Land beings,
I was also invited by the Creator Spirit
be a partner and create human Land beings.
What an event!
Human Land beings were born
in our image,
Spirit and Land united
in living creatures called human beings.

Chapter Three
The Land Custodian and the One Family Ancestral Narratives

The second Ancestral Narrative in the Bible,
heard by an ancient audience,
is about the first human beings,
'ground beings'
made of ground and breath,
who are commissioned to become
custodians
of the bushland in Eden,
the first home country
of the first humans
and who became One Family
with all the creatures
of the Land.

The Land Custodian

Narrative of Genesis 2:4–15

The First Ground Being (vv 4–9)

On the day God made the Land and the Sky, when no plant of the plains was yet on the Land and no herb of the plains had yet sprung up, because God had not caused it to rain upon the Land and there was no ground being ***to serve the ground****, but a mist rose from the Land and watered the face of the ground.*

Then God moulded ***a ground being*** *with dust from the* ***ground*** *and breathed into his nostrils the breath of life and the ground being became a* ***living being****. And God planted* ***bushlands*** *in Eden, in the East. And there he put the ground beings whom he had formed.*

And out of the ground God made to grow every tree that is pleasant to the sight and good for food; also ***the tree of life*** *in the midst of the garden and* ***the tree of the knowledge*** *of good and bad.*

The Four Rivers (vv 10–14)

A river flowed out of Eden to water the bushland and there it divided into four rivers. The name of the first is Pishon, which flows around the whole Land of Havilah, where there is gold and the gold of that Land is good; bdellium and onyx stone are also there. The name of the second river is Gihon; it is the one that flows around the whole Land of Cush. The name of the third river is Tigris, which flows East of Assyria. And the fourth river is the Euphrates.

The Mandate to Preserve the Land (v 15)

Then God took the ground being and put him in the bushland in Eden ***to 'serve' and 'preserve'*** *it.*

Analysis

The Ancestral Narrative in Genesis 2 focuses on Land beings rather than the role of the Land itself as in Genesis 1. The order of creation also differs; in Genesis 1, Land is born and gives birth to vegetation and animal life. Human beings are the last beings to emerge.

The primordial world of the narrative in Genesis 2 is a desert-like red centre watered by mist—a world devoid of all forms of life, including human beings. The only moisture is a primordial mist—rather different from the primordial waters of the Deep in Genesis 1:1–2.

Key Hebrew Terms

`adam***—frequently rendered 'man', but could better be rendered 'ground being' since the first human was made from the 'ground,' the ***`adamah. The Hebrew word for man is *`ish.*

`abad—basic meaning is to 'serve' and 'take care of' someone or something important, both in verse 5 and verse 15.

nephesh—basic meaning is 'being' as a 'living being', though in some translations it is rendered 'soul'.

gan—usually translated 'garden', but since it was filled with trees it could be rendered 'forest', or in the context of First Nations Australian culture, 'bush' or 'bushland'.

The First Ground Beings

The first 'ground being' or '*adam,* is formed or—more accurately—'moulded' by a God, who is here depicted as a potter who carefully crafts the first 'ground being' or human being. Humans are not made 'out of nothing' but from the ground of the Land: the primal source of all Land territories and all living Land beings. The root of the noun for 'man', '*adam,* can also mean 'red'. The first human being is apparently the colour of the red ground—a red man in the primordial red centre.

The 'breath of life' that animates the 'ground being' recalls the 'Wind', the spiritual Presence hovering over the primordial waters, the spiritual source that animates the Land and Land creatures in the Genesis 1 Ancestral Narrative. Humans are not only 'ground beings' in Genesis 2; they are also living beings animated by the breath/wind of the Creator Spirit. Humans are therefore spiritual ground beings or 'Land with divine breath' beings.

The 'Bushland' in Eden

The 'ground' ('*adamah)* of the Land, from which humans are moulded, is also the location where God plants trees that reflect the beauty of the Landscape and provide food for the 'ground beings'. This location is designated the '***gan***' and regularly rendered 'garden'. The focus on the trees suggests that the term could be rendered 'forest', since the term 'garden' tends to suggest a backyard garden rather than a forest.

In the context of First Nations Australian culture, however, 'bush' or 'bushland' would be a preferable translation since the bushlands not only have forest trees but also trees that provide food.

Two unique trees are also planted in the bushland: trees that represent Life and Wisdom—a spiritual dimension that is deeper than food supply or Landscape beauty. The bushland in Eden has a spiritual dimension.

The 'knowledge of good and bad' is an idiom that probably refers to Wisdom—or at least to a superior level of knowledge consciousness. Later, Eve, the first ground woman, recognises that the tree can make her wise—and it does!

No Paradise

It is significant to note, at the outset, that the bushland and Eden are separate entities. There is no bushland called Eden, but a bushland 'in Eden'. Nor does this narrative depict Eden as tantamount to Paradise. Eden is the source of the four rivers that water the bushland, not a spectacular realm called 'Paradise' where God resides in celestial splendour.

Colonial narrators and interpreters, however, have identified Eden with Paradise, a tradition that the tourism industry has exploited, as Davidson explores in detail. In the words of Davidson:

> *As Eden becomes synonymous with Paradise, biblical referents, already undergoing expansion as seen in Ezekiel, are further expanded to construct Eden as the idealised site of beauty, luxury and divine favour.*[1]
>
> *The intersections of Eden and tourism narratives reveal the need for reconceptualising the narrative.*[2]

A close reading of the narrative as it stands reveals a primal world where the first human beings are located in a bushland with ample food supplies and natural beauty, a bushland watered by four rivers from a mysterious source called Eden. There is no Paradise in this narrative. There is, however, a rich bushland—the country for the first ground beings to tend as custodians.

No YHWH

The opening line of this narrative is literally, 'on the day YHWH God made the Land and the sky . . .' The inclusion of YHWH, the colonial God of later Israelites, is easily overlooked: the common translation is 'Lord God'. We have deleted this colonial addition to the narrative in the light of clear evidence that this God, YHWH, was only revealed to Moses as their colonial divine leader many generations later.

1. Steed Vernyl Davidson, 'Lost Paradises: Tracing the Imperial Contours of Modern Tourism on Land and Peoples' in *People and Land: De-colonising Theologies,* edited by Jione Havea (Lanham, Lexington Books/Fortress Press, 2019), 20.
2. Davidson, 'Lost Paradises', 32.

In the discussion at the end of Chapter 6, the editor claims that at the time of Adam and Eve 'they began to call on the name of YHWH . . .' (Gen 4:26b).

Many academic scholars refer to Genesis 2 as the work of the so-called Yahwist editor because he liked to insert the name of Yahweh in his revision of the narrative. Nevertheless, in Genesis 2, revision by the colonial editor is very minimal: verses 16–17 are one example of his colonial hand.

To Serve as Custodians

This line (2:15) in the Ancestral Narrative preserves a pivotal tradition, the absolute opposite of the colonial mandate to dominate in Genesis1:26–28.[3] In this ancient tradition, humans are to be custodians of the Land and are to preserve it. In the colonial text of Genesis 1, they are to dominate the Land and subdue it.

As noted earlier, the vivid contrast between these two passages is quite explicit when we compare the respective verbs employed in these two passages. The verb *rada* ('rule') is the diametric opposite of the verb *'abad* ('serve') and the verb *kabash* ('subdue') is the diametric opposite of *shamar* ('preserve'). Nor should *'abad* be rendered 'till,' as some translations suggest; the first Land being is to 'care for' the Land, not necessarily till it; this is a practice common among colonial settlers with domestic gardens or ploughed paddocks.

The first ground being placed in the bushland is not a ruler over the Land, but a custodian of his country. Efforts by interpreters and theologians to harmonise these texts (Gen 1:28 & 2:15) ignore the fact that these two passages reflect two radically different worldviews—colonial and colonial-free.

Voice of the First Nations

The Voice of George Rosendale

According to George Rosendale, one of the Rainbow Spirit elders, First Nations Australians reflect the same basic nature as that of the first humans in this Ancestral Narrative: ground beings who possess both Land and Spirit:

3. Habel, *An Inconvenient Text*, Chapter 1.

> *Aboriginal culture is spiritual. I am spiritual. Inside of me is spirit and Land, both given to me by the Creator Spirit. There is a piece of Land in me and it keeps drawing me back like a magnet to the Land from which I came. The Land too is spiritual.*[4]

George Rosendale, in his unpublished study guide for Nungalinya College, observed:

> *In our Aboriginal teaching it does not say what Yiirmbal made the first man from. The important thing is that Yiirmbal gave his breath to Aborigines, his life, his spirit. In my language we call it waawu. That is why spirit is so sacred to humans because it belongs to Yiimbal.*[5]

Elders like George Rosendale hear the verb *shamar* as 'guard' or 'protect' and reflect on how they were unable to 'guard' the Land after Captain Cook came. Some Aborigines feel a sense of shame because they were unable to 'protect/preserve' their Land.

Identification

I am Adam.
I emerged as a body from ground
and was animated
when the Creator Spirit breathed
Life into my lungs.
My country was a bushland
in the Land of Eden.
I was to be a custodian,
whose role was to
'serve and preserve' the bushland
and all life in the bush
in tune with the mind
of the Creator Spirit.

---

4. Rainbow Spirit Elders, *Rainbow Spirit Theology*, 12.
5. George Rosendale, *Spirituality for Aboriginal Christians* (Casuarina: Nungalinya College, 1993), 5.

The One Family Ancestral Narrative of Genesis 2:18–25

Within this Ancestral Narrative
of the Bible,
we can retrieve a memory
about the first family
of ground beings,
and how the first human ground being
was given a partner
with whom he became
One Flesh.

A Family of Ground Beings (vv 18–20)

Then God said, 'It is not good that the ground being should be alone; I will make a suitable companion.' So, ***out of the ground,*** *God moulded every animal of the field and every bird of the sky, to see what he would name them. And whatever the human ground being named a living creature that was its name. The human being gave names to all the animals, to the birds of the sky, and every beast of the field; but for the man there was not found a suitable companion.*

One Flesh (vv 21–25)

God caused a deep sleep to fall on the human being, and while he slept God took one of his ribs and closed up its place ***with flesh.*** *And God formed a woman out of the rib which he had taken from the ground being and brought her to the ground being. Then the ground being said:*

> *At last, here is one of my kind,*
> *bone of my bones and flesh of my flesh.*
> *She shall be called '**Woman**'.*
> *because she was taken from **Man.***

That is why a man leaves his father and his mother, is united with his wife and they become ***one flesh****. And the man and his wife were both naked, but they were not ashamed.*

Analysis

Key Hebrew Terms

'adam—frequently rendered 'man', but is here rendered 'ground being' since the first human was made from the 'ground', the *'adamah.*

'ish & 'ishah—these two technical terms for 'man' and 'woman' are first mentioned here. Prior to this point, the term often rendered 'man' is *'adam,* which we have rendered 'ground being' or 'human being'.

bashar—is the basic word for flesh: a synonym for the living body of the ground being.

Naming the Family

In this narrative, the Creator Spirit is portrayed as a creator who moulds and shapes all the creatures of the animal world as a family of ground beings in the bushland to be potential partners for the first ground being. In some colonial contexts the naming process is associated with the head of the household. In Genesis 5:3, for example, Adam names his son Seth. In other contexts, however, the naming may be a communal event, as when the women of the neighbourhood named the son of Ruth (Ruth 4:17). By naming each of the animals and birds, they become part of a 'ground being' family with Adam, who was moulded in the same way as his animal family.

One Flesh

Some interpreters have tended to view the forming of a woman from the rib of the man as an emphasis on the separation of male and female. But as Havea explains, in his article associated with the colours of the ground from which all creatures are taken:

> *The narrative looks beyond the two bodies that were separated in Genesis 2:21–22. The narrative sees similar bodies in the future, women and men (people), and inscribes that they become one flesh (Gen 2:24). The prompt for this reading is the word 'flesh,' which appears at the point of separation; the rib was taken and, and its place was covered with flesh (Gen 2:21) and at the point*

> *of coming together (as 'one flesh' in Genesis 2:24), they continue to be separate bodies, but they can become 'one flesh'.*[6]

While the creation process is associated with the first human being moulded from the ground and the woman being moulded from a rib under the flesh of the 'ground man', the ultimate goal is that they become 'one flesh' or 'flesh beings'. In this tradition, both 'ground beings' are 'Land beings', who also become one with the Land—the ground from which they originate.

Voice of the First Nations

The Voice of Kevin Gilbert

Adam and Eve were born in the Garden of Eden. And they were naked and they lived with all the animals. They were all like one mob, like Blackfellas, and animals and trees. They were all one mob . . . Now, Aboriginal Eden has always stayed here, until 200 years ago, with Aboriginal People. This was our Eden. There was no sin.[7]

The Voice of Auntie Anne

As a First Nations woman, I, Auntie Anne, have often stated that Adam and Eve could not have been Aboriginal because if they were, they would have eaten the snake and not the apple. Based on this understanding, Adam and Eve would not have been the basis for *Original Sin* entering the world. As First Nations people, we believe sin first entered the world because of colonisation.

Perhaps this perspective is born out of a Western patriarchal culture that saw women as less than men and therefore this biblical narrative was used by both the Western church and society to justify the subservience of women in their society. Then through Western colonisation and Christianity this became the vehicle in which they transported their cultural views and baggage to make others—such as First Nations peoples all over the world—less than their Western women.

---

6. Jione Havea, 'The Land Has Colours', in *People and Land: De-colonising Theologies*, edited by Jione Havea (Lanham: Lexington Books/Fortress Press, 2019), 4.
7. Kevin Gilbert, 'God at the Campfire and that Christ Fella', in *Aboriginal Spirituality: Past, Present, Future,* edited by Anne Pattel-Gray (Melbourne: HarperCollins Religous, 1996), 55.

First Nations women prefer to define their relationship and partnership with their men on the basis given to them through the Law by the Creator Spirit; here we function in an egalitarian system and society.

First Nations men and women possess an affinity with the Land and, through our Spirit, we feel the heartbeat of our Mother Earth: we are inextricability bound to her for survival.

Identification

I am Eve.
I was made from a rib
that was made from the ground
when Adam was made as a ground being.
We are one flesh, made from one Land
with all the Land beings in the bushland of Eden.
We are custodians of the bushlands
and love all the trees that we hope
generations to come
will celebrate as a primal source
of goodness and grandeur.

A Colonial Addition—Genesis 2:16–17

The Tree of Knowledge Forbidden

Then YHWH God commanded the man saying, 'You may freely eat of every tree of the forest; but of the tree of the knowledge of good and bad you shall not eat, for in the day that you eat of it you will surely die'.

Anticipating the Fall

These two verses reflect the mindset of a colonial editor who inserts a second reference to the tree of the knowledge of good and bad in anticipation of the colonial version of the so-called 'Fall of Man' in Genesis 3. The congenial Creator Spirit, who commissions the first human being to serve and preserve the bushland (2:15), is suddenly portrayed as a dominant Landlord who forbids the first man to eat from one of the beneficial trees in the bushland of Eden.

For ground beings to be human beings who are expected to know how to preserve the bushlands by facilitating good care and avoiding bad treatment, the tree of the knowledge of good and bad would be a custodial asset, not a symbol or source of death. Once again, the colonial editor identifies the God who forbids eating from the tree of knowledge as the colonial God YHWH, whose identity and presence is only revealed to Moses after the burning bush incident.

Chapter Four
The Colonial Original Sin Tradition

This narrative,
heard from a colonial perspective,
is about the first human beings,
eating
from the so-called forbidden fruit,
experiencing
an opening of their eyes
and then
five cruel curses from their God,
YHWH,
who becomes equivalent to
a cruel colonial Landlord.

The Original Sin Tradition of Genesis 3

The Cunning Snake (vv 1–5)

Now ***the snake*** *was more cunning than the other creatures of the field that YHWH God had made. And the snake said to the woman, 'Did God say, "You shall not eat of any tree of the garden"?' And the woman said to the snake, 'We may eat of the fruit of the trees of the bushland, but God said, "You shall not eat of the fruit of the tree that is in the midst of the bushland, neither shall you touch it, lest you die".' But the snake said to the woman, 'You will not die! For God knows that when you eat it, your eyes will be opened and you will be like God,* ***knowing good and evil.'***

The Opening of the Eyes (vv 6–7)

When the woman saw that the tree was good for food and that it was a delight to the eyes and that the tree was to be desired to make one wise, she took of its fruit and ate; and she also gave some to her husband and he ate.

Then ***the eyes*** *of both were opened, and they knew that they were naked; and they sewed fig leaves together and made themselves aprons.*

Hiding in the Bush (vv 8–13)

Then they heard the sound of YHWH God walking in the bush in the cool of the day, and the man and his wife hid themselves from the presence of YHWH God among the trees of the bushland.

But YHWH God called to the man and said to him, 'Where are you?'. And he said, 'I heard the sound of you in the bush, and I was afraid, because I was naked and hid myself'. Then God said, 'Who told you were naked? Have you eaten of the tree which I commanded you not to eat?' The man said, 'The woman whom you gave to be with me, she gave me the fruit of the tree, and I ate'.

Then YHWH God said to the woman, 'What is this that you have done?' The woman said, 'The snake beguiled me and I ate'.

Five Cruel Curses (vv 14–19)

Then YHWH God said to the snake:
'Because you have done this,
cursed *are you more than all animals*
and more than all wild animals.
You shall travel on your belly
and you shall eat dust all the days of your life.
I will put hatred between you and the woman
and between your seed and her seed;
he shall bruise your head
and you shall bruise his heel'.

To the woman he said,
'I shall greatly multiply your pain in pregnancy,
in pain you shall bring forth children,
but your desire shall be for your husband
and ***he shall rule over you!'****.*

To the man he said,
'Because you have listened to the voice of your
wife and eaten of the tree of which I commanded
'Thou shalt not eat of it!'
***cursed is the ground** because of you!*
In toil you shall eat of it all the days of your life.
Thorns and thistle it shall bring forth to you
and you shall eat the plants of the plains.
In the sweat of your face you shall eat bread,
till you return to the ground
for out of it you were taken.
You are dust and to dust you shall return.

Expulsion from the Bush (vv 20–24)

*The man called his wife **Eve** because she was the mother of all living. And YHWH God made for the man and his wife garments of skin and clothed them.*

Then YHWH God said, 'Behold, the man has become like one of us, knowing good and evil, and now, lest he put forth his hand and take also of the tree of life, and eat and live forever . . .'

Therefore, YHWH God sent him forth from the bushland in Eden to tend the ground from which he was taken. He drove out the man; and, at the East of the bushland, he placed the cherubim, and a flaming sword that turned every way to guard the way to the tree of life.

Analysis

Key Hebrew Terms

nachash—this term is the everyday word for 'snake' (Amos 5:19), but the role of this creature in Genesis 3 has led to the widespread translation 'serpent'.

yod'e tob wara'—this idiom can be rendered 'knowing good and evil' or 'knowing good and bad'. It does not simply refer to knowing the difference between 'good and bad'; it refers to complete knowledge or wisdom.

'eynim— this is the everyday word for 'eyes' but in this context, it is a euphemism for a new level of consciousness.

'arur— from the verb ***'rr*** to curse, has the harsh meaning of being 'cursed', 'damned' and 'forever condemned'.

chavvah—Eve—her name is derived from the verb ***chayah*** to live.

radah—the same verb for 'rule' used here is also the verb for 'rule/have dominion over' living creatures in the *imago Dei* text of Genesis 1:26–28.

The Clever Snake/Serpent

The colonial version of the so-called Fall Narrative begins with a portrayal of the snake as a cunning creature who is able to trick the first humans into sinning by disobeying a command of God, their celestial Landlord. As a result, traditional translations have rendered the noun for snake *(nachash)* as 'serpent' to suggest an evil dimension of one of the good Land beings in the bush. Some theologies even associate this animal creature with the figure of Satan, a source of evil and temptation.

While the woman is aware that God has told her unequivocally that she is not to eat of the tree of the knowledge of good and evil, the 'serpent' seduces her into believing that if she eats, she will not only become 'wise'; she will also become 'like God', knowing good and evil.

The serpent, in this version, associates the knowledge of good and evil with divine wisdom; this is not a natural moral understanding of what is right and wrong in the real world. The temptation—or the 'original sin' in this version of the narrative— seems to be the desire to become 'like God' and control one's own destiny.

A New Worldview

The colonial version of Genesis 3 is a portrayal of 'original sin' as a devious desire to become a lord like the God of the bushland in Eden, to become a Landlord with divine wisdom.

When the primal pair do eat of the forbidden fruit, their eyes are indeed opened—they gain wisdom: a new level of consciousness. But in this colonial version, their wisdom is also associated with an awareness of their nakedness and a fear of their Landlord, not to their deep understanding of reality as wise Land beings.

In this colonial version, the aftermath of eating the forbidden fruit reflects a negative response to their eye-opening experience. Instead of a celebration, they have a desire to hide from their master because of a sense of shame associated with their nakedness. In this colonial text, lasting divisions are experienced between the Land beings and their God, between the man and the woman, and between the woman and the snake.

The previous peaceful world of the Land family, where the Land beings 'serve' and 'preserve' the bushland (2:15), has become a world of opposites, a colonial regime in the following order: God, man, woman, animals and ground. The original sin in this tradition creates a new worldview of colonial opposites.

Cruel Curses

The language of the curse reflects the colonial worldview of the narrator and the tradition incorporated in the script. The snake is forced to crawl on its belly and eat the dust of the ground from which it came.

The woman is destined to experience extreme pain when she gives birth, even though to become 'one flesh' was an anticipated joy. And tragically, the man will 'rule' over the woman as if she were a colonial servant in an ancient empire.

Male supremacy is identified as an enduring primordial curse.

The man, in turn, will not experience the joy of his being moulded from the 'ground'; he will discover that the very substance from which he was formed was itself to be cursed. In death, he will return to the cursed ground from which he emerged.

The five cruel curses are:

- the snake is damned to crawl on the cursed ground and eat dust
- the woman is cursed with excessive pain in childbirth
- the woman is to be 'ruled' by her husband
- the man is cursed with the need to do hard labour to produce food
- the ground itself is cursed and becomes the land of the dead.

In this colonial world, everything is cursed—everything from the ground from which the humans originate, to the ground that they are supposed cultivate, to their relationships while living on the ground, to the ground itself to which they return in death. The colonial hierarchy is clear:

YHWH God	-	the ground Landlord
the first man	-	the ground being
the first woman	-	ruled by the ground man
the serpent	-	cursed to crawl on ground
the ground	-	cursed location for the dead

In short, the colonial story of 'original sin' is tantamount to an 'original curse': a narrative that offers no hope or blessing for those who are descendants of the primal pair in the bushland of Eden, and a God who is not even ready to forgive the first ground being he has made.

Expulsion from the Bushland

The cruel treatment of the primal pair persists, even if it seems their Landlord shows some sympathy by killing some animals to provide the primal pair with 'garments of skin'.

Their God, YHWH, declares that by knowing 'good and evil', the primal pair has become 'like one of us'. It is plausible that the 'us' is the same celestial 'us' whose image humans were to reflect (Gen 1:26). This God, it would seem, seeks to protect the celestial world from invasion by ancestral humans who, having also eaten from the tree of life, could 'live forever' like celestial beings.

A colonial worldview, with YHWH as the celestial Overlord controlling the world of human beings, is very apparent in this reading. 'Knowing good and evil' is not a wisdom asset in this tradition, but a threat to the celestial world of the divine.

The Voice of the First Nations

Who would want to identify with any of these cursed creatures?

The Voice of Auntie Anne

This colonial view of a God is one that separates the Creator Spirit from creation. Is not one with which the First Nations people can relate to at all—the Creator Spirit is the centre of our universe and the life force of our Mother Earth on which all life depends for survival.

It is important to note that within First Nations society, Women's Business holds a very important and respected place. We cannot comprehend a life that is not Creator-centred. The role of First Nations women is considered critical to the maintenance, continuity and survival of the entire societal structure. First Nations society, as we knew it then and as it still is, depends on the equal participation of women.

Today, the status and position of First Nations women within Australia differs, depending upon the impact and absorption of the colonisation, missionisation and Western patriarchal beliefs in our society. This biblical interpretation and these Western values have done much to undermine the status and role of First Nations women throughout our Land.

That is why it is critical for biblical narratives to be de-colonised so that they dismantle and hopefully eradicate colonial power and domination, and will give way to the empowerment of all First Nations people around the world.

Chapter Five
The Wisdom Tree Narrative
A De-colonised Retrieval of Genesis 3

Genesis 3
heard from a de-colonised perspective,
is about the first ground beings,
eating from the Wisdom Tree—
the tree of the knowledge of good and bad—
experiencing an original
Wisdom consciousness
that enables them to be
custodians of the ground
that is blessed with fertility
and to which they return
in peace.

The Original Wisdom Tradition of Genesis 3

The Wisdom Tree (vv 1–5)

Now the snake was wiser than the other creatures of the plains that God had made. And the snake said to the woman, 'Did God say, "You shall not eat of any tree in the bush?". And the woman said to the snake, 'We may eat of the fruit of the trees in the bush, but I am not sure about the tree of the knowledge of good and bad, ***the Wisdom Tree in the midst of the bushland****. Then the snake said to the woman, 'When you eat from that tree your eyes will be opened and you will gain Wisdom, knowing what is good and what is bad'.*

The Opening of Eyes (vv 6–7)

When the woman saw that the tree was good for food and that it was a delight to the eyes and that the tree was to be desired to make one wise, she took of its fruit and ate; and she also gave some to her husband and he ate.

Then ***the eyes of both were opened****, and they knew that they were naked but they also knew that they were wise. Then they sewed fig leaves together and covered themselves.*

An Evening in the Bush (vv 8–13)

Then they heard the sound of God walking in the bush in the wind of the day; the ground being and his wife were aware of the presence of God among the trees of the bush.

Then God called to the male ground being and said to him, 'Where are you?'.

The male ground being said, 'We were hoping to meet you'. Then God said, 'Have you eaten of the Wisdom Tree in the bushland?' The ground being said, 'The woman whom you gave to be with me, she gave me the fruit of the tree, and I ate'.

God said to the woman, 'What is this that you have done?'. The woman said, 'The snake invited me and I ate'. Then God said, 'Well done! ***You have both become wise*** *and are now conscious of the realities of good and bad, a Wisdom consciousness you will need to be custodians of the bushland and to face the world beyond the bushland in Eden.'*

Five Rich Blessings (vv 14–19)

Then God said to the snake,
'Because you have done this, you are blessed,
and even though you will crawl on the ground,
you will celebrate life with all the wild animals
and with the woman who heard your voice.'

To the woman he said,
'Blessed are you, and even though you may have
pain when bring forth a child,

your baby will be a blessing,
the 'one flesh' you will celebrate with you husband.'

To the man he said,
'Blessed are you
because you have eaten from the Wisdom Tree.
Now you will have Wisdom to know what is good
and what is bad when you care for the ground.
The ground will also be blessed
and bring forth all the plants of the plains.
You will celebrate life
until you return with my spirit
to the ground from which you were moulded.'

Outside the Bush in Eden (vv 20–24)

The ground being called his wife 'Life' (Eve) because she is the mother of all life. And God made for the man and his wife garments to wear and clothed them.

Then God said, 'Behold the man is wise; he knows about good and bad. So, when he leaves the bushland in Eden to 'serve and preserve' the ground throughout the world, he will find the blessings of the ground and create life with his wife.'

Analysis

De-colonising Genesis 3

To de-colonise a biblical text such as Genesis 3 may seem presumptuous for some interpreters. After all, this chapter has long been a key text for the Christian doctrine of original sin. When listening from a First Nations' perspective, however, the current Genesis 3 version has all the earmarks of a colonial orientation—a factor that provokes us to discern and retrieve an underlying tradition that is consistent with our spiritual worldview and free of colonial editing.

Our de-colonising of this tradition, therefore, is designed to retrieve a narrative consistent with the tradition of Genesis 2 where all components of the Land family in the bush are in harmony. That one tree of the bush, or one animal in the ground family named by the first ground being, should have the potential to divide relations and destroy potential for a positive future seems to be totally inconsistent with the goodwill of the Creator Spirit in Genesis 2.

A bushland where all components play positive relational roles implies that eating from the Wisdom Tree has a valuable potential for all involved—a potential we might well designate 'original wisdom' rather than 'original sin'.

Original Wisdom

The 'opening of the eyes' after eating from the 'Wisdom Tree' means that the primordial pair of ground beings experience a radical new consciousness: a deep awareness of the basic realities of existence that may be summarised as 'the good and the bad' in this world.

This 'original wisdom' would enable the first ground beings, in cooperation with the whole family of ground beings, to be effective custodians of the bushland in which they could differentiate readily what would be good and what would be bad for the future of the bushland, their primal home Country.

A Stroll in the Bush

In the de-colonised version of this narrative, the God of the bushland is enjoying an evening stroll. When he meets with the ground beings he discovers that they have eaten from the Wisdom Tree in the bush, he celebrates the occasion. These two ground beings are now wise beings who can use their Wisdom skills to good advantage as custodians of the bush.

Five Rich Blessings

God's response to eating from the tree of the knowledge of good and bad would be one of rich blessings rather than cruel curses. The blessings would be the opposite of the five curses found in the colonial version. In the de-colonised reading, the five blessings will involve all parties: the snake, the woman, the man and the very ground from which they were all formed and to which they will return with the blessing of their Creator Spirit.

The snake will celebrate life with wild animals. The woman will celebrate the birth of a child and not be dominated by her man. She will rejoice in being one flesh with her husband. The man will celebrate the fertility of the ground and the ground itself will be blessed.

Rather than returning to the cursed ground to die a miserable death, the ground beings will return to the blessed ground as custodians with the blessing of the One who made them from the ground.

A Positive Postscript

A postscript to the story of 'original wisdom' highlights the significance of the woman as the source of life, rather than being a creature ruled by her husband as in the colonial version.

It also emphasises that the ground will not be cursed but will continue to be blessed and that the primal pair will continue to be custodians of the Land, 'serving and preserving' it as they were commissioned to do (2:15).

While the bushland in Eden may have been the original country of the first humans, their custodial Wisdom would enable them to fulfil their mission in countries outside the bushland in Eden, a feat acclaimed by God and his attendants.

The Voice of the First Nations

George Rosendale says in an unpublished workbook:

> *Look at the other verses where it says God provided for this Adam. He didn't want him to be lonely, so he provided a companion, a woman. Look at the responsibility he gave him to name all the animals. And a privilege! God could have done without him, but God said, 'No! He is my friend. I want him to be part of me'. That is the understanding Aborigines always had of Yiirmbal.*[1]

Identification

I am Eve.
In the bush in Eden
there was a special tree,
the Wisdom Tree
embracing the knowledge of good and bad.

1. Rosendale, *Spirituality for Aboriginal Christians*, 6.

When I had the courage to take
fruit from the Wisdom Tree,
my eyes were opened
and I was conscious of another world:
the world of Wisdom
and truth.

I gave some fruit to my man
and his eyes were opened too.

No matter what some critics say,
Wisdom brought many blessings
that persist
outside the bushland in Eden,
blessings that grow from the Land
to which we belong
as wise Land beings.

Chapter Six
The Cain and Abel Tradition & The Colonial God YHWH

Genesis Four,
heard from a colonial perspective,
is about Cain,
a tiller of the cursed ground
who is torn from the ground
and becomes a wanderer on the Land
because of his killing of Abel.
Cain bears a mark for his protection
while living apart from his God,
but the editor informs us
that at that time
people began to worship
YHWH.

A Colonial Cain & Abel Tradition of Genesis 4:1–26

Abel: God's Favourite (vv 1–7)

Now Adam knew his wife Eve and she conceived and bore ***Cain****, saying, 'I have* ***gained*** *a man with the help of YHWH'. And again she bore his brother Abel.*

Now ***Abel*** *was a keeper of sheep and Cain a tiller of the ground.*

In the course of time, Cain brought to YHWH an offering from the fruit of the ground. And Abel brought, from the firstborn of his flock, the fat portions.

YHWH was pleased with Abel and his offering, but he rejected Cain and his offering. Cain was very angry and his face fell.

Then YHWH said to Cain, 'Why are you angry and why has your face fallen? If you do well, will you not be accepted? And if you do not do well, sin is crouching at the door: its desire is for you, but you must master it.'

Bloody Murder (vv 8–12)

Then Cain said to his brother Abel, 'Let's go out into the fields. When they went out into the field, Cain turned on his brother and killed him.

Then YHWH asked Cain, 'Where is your brother Abel?'.

He answered, 'I don't know! Am I my brother's keeper?'

And YHWH said, 'What have you done? The voice of your brother's ***blood*** *is crying to me from the ground. Now you are cursed from the ground which has opened its mouth to receive your brother's blood from your hand. When you till the ground, it will no longer yield to you its strength; you will be a fugitive and wanderer on the Land.'*

The Fate of a Fugitive (vv 13–17, 25–26a)

Cain said to YHWH, 'My punishment is greater than I can bear. Behold you have driven me away this day from the ground; and from your face I will be hidden. I shall be a fugitive and a wanderer on the Land and whoever finds me will slay me.'

Then YHWH said, 'No! If anyone slays Cain, vengeance will be taken on him sevenfold.' And YHWH put a mark on Cain lest any who found him should kill him.

Then Cain went away from the presence of YHWH and dwelt in the Land of Nod, East of Eden.

Cain knew his wife and she conceived and bore Enoch; he built a city and called the name of the city after the name of his son Enoch.

Adam knew his wife again and she bore a son and called his name Seth, for she said, 'God has given me another child to replace Abel, whom Cain killed. To Seth also was born a son and he called his name Enosh.

The Colonial God YHWH (4:26b)

*At that time, they began to call on the **name of YHWH.***

Analysis

Key Hebrew Terms

qanah—to 'gain'; it is a wordplay on the name Cain.

hebel —the name for Abel also means 'vapour', the exact opposite of ***neshamah***, the 'breath' of God (2.7). In the beginning of the Book of Ecclesiastes, ***hebel*** is rendered 'vanity of vanities/vapour of vapours'.

dam—'blood' is here portrayed as a living or spiritual force that responds to Abel's death

Cain and Abel

Cain is portrayed as a post-Eden farmer who tills the ground, a domain that was cursed by God in the previous colonial text (Gen 3:17).

Nevertheless, Cain brings produce from his cursed ground as an offering to his God. Cain, moreover, is the first born: the one destined to bear the image of God pronounced on the first humans.

His mother, Eve, claims that the God YHWH helped her give birth and gain a son. The verb 'gain' *(qana)* is a wordplay on the name Cain.

Abel, it seems, is born without special divine assistance and with the ironic name Abel, from the noun *hebel*, which means 'vapour' or 'breath'; his name implies he is the transient one.

Nevertheless, the offering of Abel is depicted as one of higher quality than that of Cain and therefore seems to provoke a more positive response from the God to whom they make their offerings. Presumably, Cain hoped to secure God's blessing for his labours on the cursed ground.

Understandably, when Abel gets the blessing, Cain is rather annoyed and he is angry with his God. Abel seems to be God's favourite and his God a rather biased Overlord. The curse causes the ground to yield meagre harvests (Gen 3:17) that seem to have diminished the value of Cain's offering.

God's response is to advise Cain that he needs to keep his passion under control because a force called 'sin' is lying in ambush at the door, like a wild animal (*cf* Gen 49:9), to overwhelm him. The ambush by 'sin' anticipates the ambush of Cain when he kills Abel.

Bloody Murder

The killing of Abel by Cain is not portrayed in dramatic terms, but simply reported as a fact. The killing as such does not seem to be the primary concern of the colonial oriented narrator; his focus is on the consequences of the killing.

Even though the ground is cursed, it has a sympathetic relationship with Abel and channels the voice of Abel's blood. The voice, it would seem, 'screams bloody murder!' The voice of the blood suggests that in these ancient times 'blood' had a spiritual dimension.

The fate of Cain is a dual curse: Cain is 'cursed' when working the ground and the ground is cursed with infertility if Cain continues to try and till the ground. In the colonial tradition, 'cursing' is a persistent way of the colonial God YHWH to control the ground and the life on the Land.

Cursed from the Ground

The cursing of the ground not only creates a painful experience for Cain if he tries to till the ground, but also reflects a tragic sense of being expelled from the ground by God himself. Cain no longer belongs even to the cursed ground. Instead, he becomes a wanderer in a distant domain.

The Progeny of Cain

Despite being expelled from the cursed ground of his homeland, Cain has the capacity to build a city and have numerous progeny (4:18–24) who are not listed in the genealogy of Adam; Adam's progeny through Seth continue to bear the image of God (Gen 5:1ff).

The colonial curse, moreover, means that Cain lives and yet thrives without any recognition of the Presence of the God who forced him to leave the Land where he killed Abel.

The name of Adam's new son is Seth, a word that reflects the idea that he is a 'gift' of God—a gift that causes Adam's wife Eve to rejoice.

The Colonial God, YHWH

The declaration by the colonial editor that Adam and his family began to worship YHWH by calling on the name of YHWH is significant because YHWH is the name of God revealed to Moses (Exod 6:3): a God who identifies himself as the colonial God who promises Moses and his people that they will one day be able to colonise Canaan.

This closing editorial comment means that wherever the name YHWH appears in Genesis 1–11, it is a bold addition that reflects the work of a colonially oriented editor. The identification of YHWH as the colonial God of Israel is outlined in Exodus and involves several stages.

- ***Initial Identification***

In the initial identification, YHWH calls to Moses from the burning bush and identifies himself as follows:

*I **am the God of your fathers**, the God of Abraham, the God of Isaac and the God of Jacob* (Exod 3:6).

> The initial identification of YHWH is that he is the God of the Fathers, with no indication of his name as the God of the Fathers or his association with El, the Creator Spirit of Canaan.

- ***Second Identification***

Significantly, after the initial identification, Moses does not know the name of the God of Abraham, Isaac and Jacob.

> *If I come to the people of Israel and say to them, 'The God of your fathers has sent me to you', and they ask me,* **'What is his name?'** what shall I say to them? (Exod 3:13).

The dilemma Moses faces is that the traditions of the ancestors do not seem to have been preserved faithfully by the Israelites. Moses does not assume that the God of the Fathers is the God that Abraham worshipped in Canaan: El Elyon, the Creator Spirit of Canaan.

The God of Moses then provides a second identification and replies with a cryptic enigmatic answer that has long challenged interpreters.

> *And God said to Moses 'I AM WHO I AM'. Say to the people of Israel, 'I AM has sent me to you'. Then God also said to Moses,*

> *Say this to the people of Israel, '**YHWH**, the God of your fathers, the God of Abraham, the God of Isaac and the God of Jacob has sent me to you'*, (Exod 3:14–15).

The significant development is the identification of the God of the fathers as YHWH—the classic name of the God of Israel—a name that was not known to Moses and the people of Israel until the time of Moses. If the name YHWH was not known to Moses, it certainly was not known to the Abraham community or to the primordial family of Adam and Eve.

- ***Third Identification***

Moses later complains and thereafter addresses his God as YHWH,

> *Oh YHWH, why have you done evil to this people? Why did you ever send me? For since I came to Pharaoh to speak in your name, he has done evil to this people, and you have not delivered your people at all (*Exod 5:22–23).

Moses initial association with the name YHWH is extremely negative. According to Moses, speaking in the name of YHWH causes Pharaoh to introduce additional evils. In the eyes of Moses, YHWH seems to provide no solution for the people of Israel.

Unexpectedly, this tirade of Moses is followed by a third identification of YHWH as the God of the Fathers:

> *And God said to Moses, '**I am YHWH**! I appeared to Abraham, to Isaac and to Jacob as **El Shaddai**, but by the name YHWH I did not make myself known to them. I also established my covenant with them to give them the Land of Canaan, the Land in which they dwelt as sojourners'* (Exod 6:2–4).

In this text, YHWH identifies himself with El, the Canaanite Creator Spirit, the God that the fathers knew. The name YHWH is explicitly absent from the Abraham traditions. The God, YHWH, in spite of his subsequent revelation to Moses, claims to have been the God, El—the God that Abraham and the Peoples of Canaan worshipped. . .unknowingly.

- ***Colonial Identification***

Having revealed himself to be YHWH who made a covenant that the Israelites could settle in the Land of Canaan, where he was worshipped by the Canaanites, YHWH now identifies himself not only as a saviour of the Israelites, but also identifies himself as the colonial Landowner.

> *I will bring you to the Land that I swore to give to Abraham, to Isaac and to Jacob; I will give it to you* ***as a possession****. I am YHWH* (Exod 6:8).

YHWH explicitly identifies himself as the one who will give the Israelites colonial possession of the Land of Canaan. The colonial image of YHWH is now explicit.

This image is intensified in chapters that follow. At Mt Sinai, YHWH claims to own all the Earth and chooses the Israelites to be his very own people, despite the tradition that there were peoples who also worshipped him as El, back in Canaan.

> *If you will obey my voice and keep my covenant, you shall be my very own possession among all the peoples, for all the Earth is mine* (Exod 19:5).

Finally, YHWH makes it clear that he will destroy all the peoples of Canaan, so that the Israelites can colonise the Land.

> *When my angel goes before you and brings you into the Amorites, the Perizzites, the Hittites, the Canaanites and the Jebusites,* ***I will blot them . . . I will send terror before you*** *and I will throw into confusion all the people against whom you will come. . . Little by little I will drive them out from before you until you are increased and possess the Land* (Exod 23:23–33).

The image is now clear: YHWH will destroy the peoples of Canaan and enable Israel to colonise the Land of Canaan.

This detailed identification of YHWH as the colonial God of Israel happens later, during Israelite history, and not in the primordial days of Adam.

The name of the deity worshipped by the primal ancestors remains a mystery; the editor informs us that his name was YHWH, a blatant anachronism. Wherever the name YHWH appears, we have evidence that there is a colonial narrator who has edited the tradition.

Voice of the First Nations

Voice of Auntie Anne

As a First Nations woman, I struggle with this colonial narrative that portrays a Colonial God who favours one race over another because this tradition has been used to justify Western colonisers who identify themselves as the 'Chosen Ones'. I cannot believe that this Colonial God is one and the same as the Creator Spirit that we know and understand, and in whose spirit we breathe.

This Colonial God is hell bent on destroying First Nations peoples because we could not tolerate bearing the image of this God; nor could we find comfort in, or communion with, a God who acted like a Colonial Landlord. It is imperative that by returning to the images of Creator Spirit prevalent in the culture and spirituality of the First Nations peoples of Australia, we are able to de-colonise this colonial God as we de-colonise the narratives of Genesis.

The First Nations people's faith has been nurtured over thousands of years and as a result we have a very intimate relationship with the Creator Spirit. When we speak of this relationship, we invoke the Spirit Creator in our midst.

Our Ancestral Narratives reflect this relationship and our ceremonies give praise to our Creator and remind us of our obligations to one another, to the Land and the environment, to law and the responsibilities given to us by the Creator Spirit.

Our image of God is unlike the one portrayed by many missionaries, who presented God as dwelling at a distance, living in heaven in splendid isolation. Many early missionaries did not discern either that God was present in the Land of Australia, or the high level of spirituality that was present in our Aboriginal culture long before they appeared.

Chapter Seven
A Colonial & an Anti-colonial *imago Dei Tradition*

Genesis 1–11
includes a series of genealogies
that record ancient male ancestors of humankind,
ranging from Adam to Abraham.
A significant colonial dimension
of these genealogies is prefaced
in Genesis 5:1–2
with a reference to the earlier
imago Dei tradition,
indicating that the likeness of God
is continued in sons who bear
the likeness of their parents.
After the initial genealogy,
the narrator has included
a brief story (6:1–4)
which is essentially
a bold critique
of the imago Dei tradition.

1. Generations of the Image in Genesis 5:1–32, 10:2–3, 11:10–30

Sons in the Likeness of their Fathers (vv 1–5)

This is the Book of the Generations of Adam. When God created humans, he made them in the likeness of God. Male and female he created them and blessed them and named them 'Humans' when he created them.

> *When Adam had lived 130 years, he became the father of a son in his own likeness, in his image, and named him Seth. The days of Adam after he became the father of Seth were 800 years; and he had other sons and daughters. All the days that Adam lived were 930 years; and he died.*

The Patriarchal Genealogies

***Genealogy 1:* Genesis 5:2–32**

Adam: Genesis 5:2–5
Seth: Genesis 5:6–8
Enosh: Genesis 5:9–11
Kenan: Genesis 5:12–14
Mahalel: Genesis 5:15–17
Jared: Genesis 5:18–20
Enoch: Genesis 5:21–24
Methuselah: Genesis 5:25–27
Lamech: Genesis 5:28–31

***Genealogy 2:* Genesis 10:2–31**

Japheth: Genesis, 10:2–5
Ham: Genesis 10:6–14
Canaan: Genesis 10:15–20
Shem: Genesis 10:21–31

***Genealogy 3*: Genesis 11:10–30**

Shem: Genesis 11:10–11
Arpachshad: Genesis 11:12–13
Shelah: Genesis 11:14–15
Eber: Genesis 11:16–17
Peleg: Genesis 11:18–19
Reu: Genesis 11:20–21
Serug: Genesis 11:22–23
Nahor: Genesis 11:24–25
Terah: Genesis 11:26–30

Analysis

The imago Dei Link

The preface to the books of the generation of the primal ancestors recorded in Genesis 1–11 makes an explicit link with the *imago Dei* colonial text of Genesis 1:26–28. The connections are made in three ways:

- humans are made in the 'likeness of God'
- created 'male and female'
- 'blessed' with a primordial blessing.

Here the *imago Dei* is recorded as singular, 'the image of God'— even though, in the text of the original *imago Dei* passage in Genesis 1:26–28, the expression 'let us' seems to suggest a reference to the council of divine beings and that the image refers to 'the image of the gods'.

Even though the original text speaks of 'male and female', the genealogical records focus exclusively on the male colonial line of the ancestors.

Ancestral Beings

The extreme lifespan of these ancestors suggests that they are ancestral beings unlike later human beings. As such they may be viewed as similar to the ancestral beings that preceded human beings according to the Ancestral Narratives of First Nations Australia. In the anti-*imago Dei* narrative that follows (in Gen 6:1–4), this discrete Ancestral Being nature seems to be confirmed when God reduces future generations to normal human beings with reduced life spans. Initially the ancestral beings allegedly lived, as did Adam, for almost a thousand years.

Significantly these genealogical records conclude with Terah, the father of Abraham—a key figure in several relevant biblical traditions found in Genesis 12–25 that are free from colonial influence.

2. A Critique of the *imago Dei Tradition* in Genesis 6:1–4

Ancestral Beings Reduced to Mortal Humans

> *When the ancestral ground beings began to multiply on the face of the ground and daughters were born to them, the sons of the gods saw that the daughters of the ground beings were beautiful and they selected wives from them as they chose.*
>
> *Then the Creator Spirit said, 'My spirit shall not abide in ancestral ground beings forever, for they are flesh; their days will be 120'.*
>
> *The Nephilim were on the Land in those days and also afterwards when the sons of the gods came to the daughters of the ground beings and they bore children to them. These were the heroic ones of old, men of renown.*

Analysis

The Nephilim Legend

The plot of the so-called Nephilim legend of Genesis 6:1–4 can be outlined as follows:

- setting: among the ancestral ground beings *('adam)* who multiplied on the ground (*'adamah*)
- catalyst: the sensual divine beings take wives from among the women of the ancestral ground beings
- response: God declares that the ancestral ground beings are to be deprived of their ancestral 'spirit' and become mortal human beings, living for only 120 years
- closure: Nephilim, the progeny of the fallen divine men and ancestral wives, also live on the ground.

This brief narrative, often been viewed as a Preface to the following ancestral Flood narratives, provides an alternative rationale for the devastation of the Land by the flood waters. A close analysis of the language and text of this narrative plot, however, reveals a close connection with the preceding image tradition: the colonial *imago Dei* text of 1:26–28, rather than the subsequent Flood Tradition.

The narrative opens with a direct reference to the colonial blessing of 1.28 when God says, 'be fruitful and multiply and fill the Land and subdue it'.

According to the narrator of Genesis 6:1–4, ancestral ground beings did multiply and fill the Land, but are not reported as having 'ruled' the animal world or having 'subdued the Land'. Instead, they are portrayed as a community of 'spirit filled' Ancestral Beings with beautiful women whom the divine beings find sexually appealing.

Ancestral Ground Beings and Divine Beings

We have translated ***'adam*** as 'ground beings' rather than 'men'. They are also Ancestral Beings who lived for up to a thousand years—not the normal lifespan of humans.

The reference to divine beings—or more specifically 'sons of the gods'—immediately suggests another link with the 'us' in the *imago Dei* narrative of Genesis 1:26–28, which begins, 'Then God said, "Let *us* make human beings in *our* image, in *our* likeness"'.

In making his original recommendation (Gen 1:26), God addresses his company of fellow divine beings as 'us'; the image to be projected on the new beings is not 'my image' but 'our image'. So, speaking of *imago Dei* as referring exclusively to God, as most theologies do, is inconsistent with this text. A more accurate rendering would be *imago divinae,* the image of divine beings.

Celestial Intercourse

When the divine beings, living with God above, view the ancestral ground beings below, they discern 'spirit filled' beings who bear the *imago divinae* and find them logical divine image partners, selecting whomever they choose.

The response of this God to the intercourse between the ancestral ground beings and the divine beings may at first seem strange. We might expect God to punish the divine beings for their bold interference in the lives of the female ground beings.

We may, however, discern that bearing 'our divine image' may well imply the potential for the ancestral humans to be immortal like the celestial divine beings. If so, it then makes sense that God decides to end the interplay of beings in 'our image' and reduce the ancestral ground beings to mortal human beings by removing the divine 'spirit' they possess.

Accordingly, God limits the lives of the ancestral 'spirit filled' ground beings to 120 years; they are devoid of their previous ancestral 'spirit'. Presumably, these mortal human beings would have a different image and not be as appealing to divine beings.

The Nephilim

For the ancient audience of this critique of the so-called *imago Dei* tradition, the prevailing legends about giant Nephilim on the Land would provide local evidence that the narrative was worth remembering. The name 'Nephilim', by the way, is probably intended to be satirical; the name probably means 'miscarriages'.

An additional critique of the *imago Dei* tradition is the fact that the perverts from the celestial council are not reprimanded or punished for their actions. Instead, the very ancestral beings—who were supposed to reflect the celestial *imago divinae*—are reduced to human mortals whose lives are limited to 120 years.

> *It is striking, however, that the party that violated the boundaries between heaven and Earth is not affected in any way. It is the humans, not the sons of Elohim, who experience God's response. As with the cursing of 'adamah (ground) when Adam sins, a party other than the culprit suffers.*[1]

A Bold Critique?

This narrative may well be interpreted as an early critique of the *imago Dei* tradition, a narrative with a measure of satire that can be summarised:

- filling the Land with ancestral ground beings who are not identified as mortal but are potentially immortal
- exposing the *imago Dei* as, in fact, *imago divinae*, referring to the 'us' of the original divine word and the 'divine beings' as those who have intercourse with the ancestral ground beings
- the action of God rendering the potentially immortal 'spirit filled' ancestral beings into mortal human beings
- the allusion to the Nephilim as legendary evidence to support this revised narrative.

Ultimately, then, this critique is a way of declaring that humans are no longer beings in the image of the gods, a factor that would have made them eternal like the gods. Without the *imago Dei*, they are human beings in the image of the Land *(imago terrae*), a factor that makes them mortal.

Voice of the First Nations

The Voice of Auntie Anne

I can remember as a young woman reading this narrative and getting really excited by it because it affirmed for me my people's understanding of our world. The Creator Spirit interacted with our Spirit Ancestors in the creation of our being and our world; our ancestors were like the Nephilim.

This gave me great joy as I felt the Creator Spirit touch my very soul and I knew that the Creator Spirit was one and the same as the Creator Spirit depicted in our oral Ancestral Narratives.

---

1. Norman Habel, The *Birth, the Curse and the Greening of Earth* (Sheffield: Sheffield Phoenix Press, 2011), 80.

Identification

I am a giant Nephilim,
an ancient legendary figure
who roamed the Land in the days of Noah—
or so people said.

You may think the name Nephilim
means fallen or miscarriage,
that we are fallen angels or monsters.

Far from it!
We are amazing beings,
the progeny of the divine beings above
and the ancestral beings below,
who, because they were created
in the image of the gods above,
were destined to be eternal,
beautiful and bold—or so they were told.

The gods were enchanted
by these beautiful new beings
and enjoyed creating progeny,
one of whom is I.
Do you believe me?

Chapter Eight
The Two Flood Narratives

It has long been recognised
by biblical interpreters
that Genesis 6–9
is a combined arrangement of
two discrete flood narratives:
one associated with
the so-called Yahwist editor
and the other with
the so-called Priestly editor;
one with limited colonial editing
and the other with
a consistent colonial orientation.
In the chapter that follows
the narratives of these two discrete traditions
will be translated,
analysed,
and their colonial editing identified.

Identifying The Two Flood Narratives

The parallel features of these two versions of the flood narrative are summarised in the following table.

The Two Flood Narratives: Summary of Key Ideas	
So-called Yahwist Version	***So-called Priestly Version***
Rationale As in Genesis 2–3, God is portrayed in human terms. Humans and their Land are his concern, but humans are now viewed as wicked and something must be done. God grieves. Then one man finds favour.	***Rationale*** As in Genesis 1, the Land is a central concern of God, but now God views Land itself as corrupt, and needs to be destroyed, along with all flesh. One man is chosen to make a covenant with God.
Divine Instructions Noah is to take 7 of each of the clean animals into an ark and 2 each of the unclean.	***Divine Instructions*** Noah is to build an ark according to God's design and take 2 of each species into the ark.
Nature of the Flood God sends rain (showers) that produces a flood capable of lifting the ark off the Land.	***Nature of the Flood*** God causes the fountains of the deep and the windows in the sky to burst open and inundate the Land; even the mountains disappear.
Duration of the Flood The rain and flooding last 40 days and 40 nights. Noah waits three weeks before disembarking.	***Duration of the Flood*** A full cycle of 12 months (or 1 year and 10 days) passes before creation is restored to order and the Land is dry.
Conclusions	
***Conclusion One*: 8:20–22** God is again viewed in human terms, smelling the sacrifice, talking to himself, and making a promise	***Conclusion Two:* 9:1–7** God reiterates the mandate for humans to dominate all living creatures who now fear humans
***Conclusion Three*: 9:8–17** God makes a treaty never again to destroy the Land and all flesh. The rainbow is his sign.	

The Editing of the Two Flood Legends

The separation of the two flood legends into the categories of Yahwist and Priestly editing is based on a technique of classical literary or source criticism. A detailed analysis of this literary division is found in my text, *Literary Criticism of the Old Testament*.[1] In this study I identified the distinguishing features of the Yahwist and Priestly editors identified by biblical scholars, including their style, terminology, idioms and theology. With reference to the divine names, the Yahwist regularly used the name YHWH or YHWH Elohim, while the Priestly writer used the name Elohim, a standard Hebrew word meaning 'God'.

Both versions of this traditional oral legend from the distant past, edited by two narrators living in the colonial world of ancient Israel, were then combined into the biblical narrative we now have, resulting in a complex Flood Narrative embracing two ancient Flood traditions edited by two discrete narrators.

The issue we now face is how to:

- discern the colonial editing of both the narrators
- highlight the discrete features that each of these narrators captures in his editing of the Flood tradition
- retrieve, where possible, ancient memories in the narrative that may be free from colonial elaboration.

The translations and analyses that follow in Chapter 9 do not focus on the classic literary features that distinguish these two versions of the flood legend. Using our de-colonising reading strategies, we will explore the overt colonial features of the narratives to ascertain whether we can retrieve a de-colonised Flood tradition that is free from colonial editing and ascertain its relevance for the First Nations listeners and readers of Australia and beyond.

1. Norman Habel, *Literary Criticism of the Old Testament* (Philadelphia: Fortress Press, 1971).

Chapter Nine
A De-colonised and A Colonial Flood Narrative

In a de-colonised Flood narrative
we retrieve the ancient tradition
that lies behind the so-called
Yahwist version of the Flood
and we hear the story of how
the Creator Spirit
restores the Land
to its original vitality.

In the colonial Flood narrative
we highlight the colonial tradition
that lies behind
the Priestly version of the Flood
and we hear how
God plans to destroy the Land
because it is corrupt.

1. A De-colonised Flood Narrative Cleansing the Land with Flood Waters

The First Flood narrative,
retrieved from what has
usually been designated
the Yahwist Version,
has a strong pre-colonial orientation.

The Flood is provoked by God,
because humans damaged
the primordial Landscape

and the Creator,
who becomes anxious,
devises a plan
to restore the Land
by sending a Flood of cleansing waters
allowing Noah
and two of each species of living creatures
to survive
and be blessed.

The First Flood Narrative Retrieved from Genesis 6–8

Divine Anguish (6:5–8)

The Spirit of the Creator Spirit was present in the Land since the time the Land emerged from the primordial Deep and became a dynamic fertile mother of many Land beings.

Over time, many of the Land beings—including human Land beings—became violent and damaged the pristine primordial Landscape. As a result, the Creator Spirit became distraught and devised a plan to restore the Land to its primal virility.

The faithful family of Noah was chosen to be part of that plan: cleansing the Land with a Flood.

Cleansing Rains (7:1–5)

The Creator Spirit said to Noah, 'I want you to construct an ark in which you can live during the Flood I have planned. Take with you two of each species of living creatures, both male and female.

In seven days I will send cleansing rain upon the Land, for 40 days and 40 nights; and every living being that has been corrupted I will destroy and I will *rejuvenate the Land.'*

Noah did all that Creator Spirit commanded him.

The Advent of the Flood (7:7–20, 12, 16–17, 22–23)

Noah and his sons, his sons' wives and two of each species of living creature went into the ark to escape the waters of the Flood, as God had commanded. Then the Creator Spirit, hovering over the Land, shut the door of the ark for Noah.

After seven days, the waters of the Flood came upon the Land. The Flood continued 40 days on the Land; and the waters increased and bore up the ark and it rose high above the Land. Everything on the dry Land in whose nostrils were the breath of life died.

Life inside the Ark (8:6–12, 13b)

At the end of 40 days, Noah opened the windows of the ark that he had made and sent forth a raven. It went to and fro until the waters were dried up from the Land. Then he sent forth a dove to see if the waters had subsided from the face of the ground, but the dove had no place to set her foot and she returned to him in the ark for the waters were still on the face of the whole Land. Then he put forth his hand and took her and brought her into the ark with him. He waited another seven days and again he sent forth the dove out of the ark. And the dove came back to him in the evening and lo, in her mouth was a freshly plucked olive leaf; then Noah knew the waters had subsided and the Land was coming back to life. He waited another seven days and sent forth the dove and she did not return to him anymore.

Then Noah removed the covering of the ark and looked and behold the Landscape was being restored.

The Promise of Restoration (8:20–22)

Then Noah built an altar for the Creator Spirit to enjoy. The aroma from the altar pleased the Creator Spirit and he said in his heart, 'Never again will I purge the Land because of what human beings do. I will restore the Land to its primal goodness.'

> *As long as the Land exists,*
> *there will be a time for planting*
> *and a time for harvest.*
> *There will always be cold and heat,*
> *summer and winter, day and night,*
> *for my Spirit will be present*
> *in the Land. . .at all times.*

Analysis

The Tragic Pre-Flood Scenario

In a de-colonised version of the Flood narrative:

- God is the original Creator Spirit not the colonial God, YHWH
- the Creator Spirit is distraught because the Land, in which his Spirit resides, has been damaged by violence
- the Creator Spirit considers a plan to purge the Land and restore its primal goodness
- one family is chosen to survive and be part of the plan of restoration.

The Advent of the Flood

In a de-colonised version of the Flood narrative, the Creator Spirit has a positive relationship with the Land and the Land beings. His concern is to restore the Land rather than to annihilate it. The Flood is not primarily a vehicle of total destruction but of purging and restoration.

Prior to the advent of the Flood, Noah, his family and the designated living creatures, all enter the ark and wait seven days. God's personal concern for Noah is reflected in a surprising touch: the Creator Spirit shuts the door of the ark Noah has constructed! At this moment in the narrative, the Creator Spirit is present in the Land with Noah—not in the heavens above.

In this version of the Flood narrative, the Flood is caused by 40 days and 40 nights of rain—enough flooding to purge the Landscape and to lift the ark high above the Land.

Life inside the Ark

At this stage of a tragic Flood narrative, we are privileged to discern a delicate touch that tends to reveal a heart-warming dimension to an otherwise cruel portrayal of animal demise and devastation. Noah has a positive personal relationship with the birds on board, notably, the raven and the dove that are part of the family of living Land beings.

The interplay between the birds and the flooded Landscape illustrates a deep concern for the Land to once again be accessible and viable for a normal life on the Land. The birds are the messengers of peace and future hope for the Land and the inhabitants of the Land.

The Promise

In this, the first of the three conclusions to the Flood narratives, Noah builds an altar and celebrates. The Flood is over and his family joins in a feast. The Creator Spirit participates by smelling the aroma from the altar and rejoicing in his heart. His anguish has been alleviated.

The response of the Creator Spirit is to promise, not only to refrain from sending another Flood, but also to restore the fertility of the Land with a guarantee of regular times and seasons for planting and harvest in the Land.

The Voice of the First Nations

There are numerous flood legends around the world and among the Aboriginal peoples of Australia. One such story is The Bundaba Flood Story, as told by Jimmy Bird.

> *Long, long ago there was a great flood. It originated from the fact of some children who found the 'winking' owl in a tree and plucked out all its feathers. They forced a grass reed through its nose and treated the bird most shamefully. The bird flies without wings into the heavens and showed himself to Ngowungu, the Great Father. Ngowungu became angry and decided to drown the people.*
>
> *Later the people saw a small cloud rising which grew bigger and bigger till it spread over the sky. The thunder began to roll and crash and the people were greatly afraid.*
>
> *With the rain and thunder was a terrible wind which broke great limbs off trees and rooted up others. During this terrible storm there was a noise above the awful crashes of thunder. This noise was coming from the North. The salt water, the sea, came pouring over the ranges from the North. The flood rose higher and higher till all the Land was covered except for the tops of two or three mountains.*
>
> *From further west a man and his wives with a dog were battling their way in a canoe when a bird with a leaf in its mouth flew in front of them showing them the way to Mt Broome. They eventually reached Mt Broome and landed where some other survivors were.*

> *Then, Djabalgari, the great left-handed man, incised his little finger and let the blood trickle down into the flood waters. The waters began to go down and eventually disappeared off the country. All other people were drowned.*[1]

The purpose of adding this Flood narrative at this point is not to compare this story with the features of the biblical stories, but to illustrate that we First Nations peoples have told comparable stories about the Flood and numerous other narratives that relate to the Land, narratives we call Ancestral Narratives. We can therefore read a de-colonised version of the Flood narrative in the Bible as an Ancestral Narrative like our own.

Identification

I am the Dove.
I watched in deep trauma
as a flood of massive waters
rose above the trees and one by one
every animal, bird and butterfly
gasped and drowned.

A few of us who survived
alighted on a wooden boat
and were invited in by an old bloke
called Noah.

After forty days of violent rains,
old Noah sent me out of a hole
to view the Landscape.
All I could see was floating carcases.
There was no place to land
and enjoy being a bird.

After several trips I finally found
an olive tree rising from the Land.
The Land was being born again,
restored to its primal vitality,
and we could leave the old boat,
meet up with fellow Land beings
and be a family at peace once again.

---

1. Jimmy Bird, 'The Bundaba Flood Story', in *Australia Aboriginal Flood Stories*, collected by W Douglas & Howard Coates. *Creation*, 5, (1982): 2.

2. A Colonial Flood Narrative: Submerging the Land Back in the Deep

The second Flood narrative,
usually designated the Priestly Version,
has a strong colonial orientation.
The Flood is provoked
by the corruption of the Land,
caused by human violence.
The Flood that this God plans
is designed
to annihilate all living beings
and submerge the Land
in the primal waters of the Deep.
Noah, his family,
and representatives of all species,
escape
in an ark cleverly designed
by God himself.

The Second Flood Narrative of Genesis 6–8

Decision to Destroy the Land (6:9–13)

These are the generations of Noah. Noah was a righteous man, blameless among his contemporaries. And Noah walked with God. And Noah had three sons: Shem, Ham, Japheth.

Now the Land was ***corrupt*** *in God's sight and the Land was full of* ***violence****. God saw the Land and behold it was corrupt, for all flesh had corrupted its way on the Land.*

Then God said to Noah, 'I have determined to make an end of all flesh, for ***the Land is filled with violen****ce through them. Behold I will annihilate them* ***with the Land.***

Concerning the Ark (6:14–22)

'Make yourself an ark of resinous wood. Make it with weeds and cover it with pitch inside and out. This is how you are to make it: the length of the ark is 300 cubits, its breadth is 50 cubits and its height is 30 cubits. Make a roof for the ark and finish it to a cubit above, and set the door on its side. Make it with first, second and third decks.

For my part, I am bringing a flood of waters on the Land to ***annihilate all flesh*** *in which is the breath of life under the sky. But I will establish my covenant with you, and you will go on board the ark: you, your sons, your wife and your sons' wives with you.*

And from every living being of all flesh, two of each species you will bring aboard the ark, to save their lives with yours; they must be male and female. From the birds according to their species, from every creeping being according to its species, two of every species shall come in for you to keep them alive.

And take with you every sort of food that is eaten and store it up for you and for them. Noah did as God commanded him.

The Deep Bursts Open (7:6,11,13–16)

Noah was 600 years old when the flood waters came upon the Land. In the 600th year of Noah's life, in the second month, on the seventeenth day of the month, on the very day, all the fountains of the great **Deep** *burst forth and the windows of the skies were opened.*

On the very same day, Noah and his sons, Shem, Ham and Japheth, and Noah's wife and the three wives of his sons went with them. They boarded the ark, they and every beast according to its species and all the animals according to their species and everything that creeps on the Land, according to its species and every bird according to its species, every bird of every sort. They boarded the ark with Noah: two and two of all flesh in which was the breath of life. And those that boarded, male and female from all flesh, entered as God had commanded him.

The Waters Prevail (7:18–21, 24)

The waters prevailed and increased greatly and the ark went upon the face of the waters. The waters prevailed exceedingly on the Land and covered all the mountains which are under all the skies. The waters prevailed above the mountains, covering them 15 cubits deep and all flesh expired that moved on the Land: birds, animals, beasts, all swarming creatures that swarm on the Land and every human being. And the waters prevailed on the Land 150 days.

The End of the Flood (8:1–2a, 4–5, 13a, 14–19)

Then God remembered Noah and all the beasts and all the animals that were with him on the ark. And God made a ***wind*** *blow on the Land and the waters subsided. And the fountains of* ***the Deep*** *and the windows of the sky were closed.*

At the end of 150 days the waters had abated. And in the seventeenth day of the second month the ark came to rest on the mountains of Ararat. The waters continued to abate until the tenth month; and in the tenth month, the first day of the month, the tops of the mountain were seen.

In the 601st year, in the 1st month, on the first day of the month, the waters were dried up from the Land. In the second month, on the twenty-seventh day of the month, the Land was dry.

God ordered Noah, 'Go out from the ark, you and your wife, and your sons and your sons' wives with you. Bring forth with you every living being that is with you of all flesh—birds, animals and every creeping creature that creeps on the Land—that they may breed abundantly and be fruitful and multiply on the Land.

Noah went forth, and his sons and his wife and his sons' wives with him. And every beast, every creeping thing, and every bird, everything that moves upon the Land, went forth by families from the ark.

Analysis

Key Hebrew Terms

shachat—a frightening verb that can mean 'ruin', 'become corrupt', or even 'destroy'.

chamas—refers to 'violent' or 'ruthless' treatment that causes damage and danger.

tehom—the primordial 'Deep' of Genesis 1:2 that existed before the Land appeared above the Deep.

ruach—the 'wind' or 'spirit' in Genesis 1:2—the 'wind of God'.

The Violent Pre-Flood Scenario

The pre-Flood scenario in the second Flood narrative is one of relentless violence and corruption:

- this Creator God decides that creation is corrupt
- he views the corruption of the Land as absolute

- this colonial God plans to exterminate all flesh
- this colonial God plans to annihilate the Land
- one man and his family find favour.

Who is this Creator God who, soon after the acts of creation, has allowed human beings to become 'corrupt' beings and corrupt the Land?

This God is even ready to annihilate all his created beings, kill innocent animals and annihilate the Land.

This Creator God is nothing like the Creator Spirit of the First Nations Australians who is present in the Land with the living beings guiding and sustaining them. This God sounds like a colonial God who is willing to eliminate the first creation and begin again.

In this, the second Flood narrative, the decision of God is not only to destroy human beings, but also to destroy the Land, the core of creation. The Land, which humans in the colonial tradition are expected to 'subdue' (Gen 1:28), has not only been subdued but has also been 'corrupted'. In the eyes of this God, the Land is no longer a location for living beings to exist and flourish.

Noah is to be rescued from the Flood because he alone seems to have been blameless in his generation.

Concerning the Ark

In this version of the Flood narrative, Noah only takes two of every species of living creatures, while in the first Flood narrative Noah is expected to take seven of all clean species. In addition, Noah is now expected to collect the necessary food to feed all living beings on board the ark.

Noah is given all the carpentry details to construct the ark according to precise divine measurements which Noah follows to the letter.

Return to the Primordial

A significant feature of this Flood narrative is that the fountains of the Deep burst open and the Land is submerged in the waters of the Deep. The situation is a return to the primordial world of Genesis 1:2 with the Land submerged in the waters of the Deep.

In addition, the skies that once separated the waters above from the waters below (on Day 2), also burst open and the primordial world of the Deep waters returns.

In this Flood narrative, the narrator portrays the Flood as the vehicle for God to reverse the original creation process and return the world to the primordial. What then is needed is a 'new creation'. It almost seems as if this colonial narrator seeks to revoke the colonial-free narrative of Genesis 1 and introduce a transformed creation that is free from corruption.

In this world of primordial waters, Noah enters an ark, together with his family and representatives of all living creatures. With the Land submerged beneath the Deep, Noah's ark hovers on the surface waters of the Deep in much the same ways as the 'spirit of God' hovers over the primordial waters.

The Primordial Waters Prevail

The momentous dimensions of the Flood in this Flood tradition become apparent when the waters from the Deep and the waters from the skies submerge the Land so that even the mountains are submerged in the Deep. As a result, all life on the Land is annihilated.

In this version of the Flood narrative, the total course of events extends for twelve months and ten days.

The Flood Calendar

This Flood narrative provides a detailed calendar relating to Noah's life for the major moments of the Flood:

- Year 600, month 2, Day 17—the Deep bursts open, waters flood the Land and Noah enters the ark
- Year 600, month 7, Day 17—the ark rests on the mountains of Ararat
- Year 601, month 1, Day 1—New Year's Day—the waters dry up on the Land
- Year 601, month 2, Day 27—the Land is dry and Noah leaves the ark, one year and ten days after entering.

This account of the end of the Flood provides a colonial calendar that relates how God controls the course of events in the progression of the Flood—from the bursting open of the waters in the Deep to the final day when the waters have not only abated, but the Land appears, now dry enough for the inhabitants of the ark to return to the Land.

It is significant that the tradition of the primordial realm found in the colonial-free Ancestral Narrative of Genesis 1.1–2 must also have been appropriated by the colonial editor of the Second Flood narrative that includes not only the primordial waters of the Deep but also the 'Wind' of God blowing over the waters.

Return to the Land, however, is also associated with the mandate of the *imago Dei* tradition in Genesis 1:26–28. All those living beings who leave the ark in pairs are commissioned again 'to be fruitful and multiply'. The mandate for humans to have colonial dominion is confirmed in the conclusion which follows (9:1–6), a mandate that creates an even more forceful dominion than previously: all living creatures will be afraid of human beings (See Chapter 10).

The Voice of the First Nations

The First Nations people of Australia have many Ancestral Narratives that talk about a time when the Land was flooded and all of creation was destroyed, except for a few that survived. These stories have been told over the centuries by our people. The rationale for these narratives was that we learn to listen to the Creator Spirit about how to care for the precious gift of the Land that has been bestowed on us, how to maintain the laws of the Land, how to carry out ceremony, and how to live at one with creation.

The Creator Spirit taught First Nations people in Australia that we are born of the Land, our identity is one with our birthplace, and we are to be one with creation because our survival and sustainability is dependent on our relationship with the Land.

Chapter Ten
Confirmation of the *imago* *Dei* The Mandate to Dominate Intensified

The second conclusion
to the Flood narrative
confirms the divine commission
to dominate
all living Land beings on the Land
found in the original imago Dei *text*
of Genesis 1:26–28,
but adds a mandate
to respect
the lifeblood of humans
made in the image of the gods.

A Colonial Text—Genesis 9:1–7
Colonise the Land and the Land Beings

The Mandate to Dominate (vv 1–3)

God blessed Noah and his sons and said, 'Be fruitful and multiply and fill the Land. ***The fear of you and the dread of you*** *will be upon every animal of the Land, and upon every bird of the air, upon everything that creeps upon the ground and all the fish of the sea; into your hand they are delivered. Everything that moves will be food for you, and as I gave you the green plants, I now give you everything.*

Respect the Image of God (vv 4–7)

Only you shall not eat flesh with its life, that is, its blood. For your lifeblood I will require a reckoning; of every beast I will require it and of every human being; of each person's brother I will require the life of a human being. Whoever sheds blood of a human being, by a human being his blood will be shed; for God made human beings in his image. And you, be fruitful and multiply, bring forth abundantly on the Land and multiply on it.

Analysis

This text is a bold colonial portrayal of God repeating the primal announcement of God that human Land beings are to have dominion over all living beings and to subdue the Land (Gen 1:26–28). The post-Flood announcement—or more precisely mandate—differs from the original mandate in several significant ways that heighten the colonial control of human beings.

1. ***Colonise and Terrify!***

This God clearly gives human beings, represented here by Noah and his family, the power and the authority to dominate all living creatures—whether they inhabit the Land, water or air. The sovereignty of humans persists, despite the fact that the animal world suffers unjustly in the flood. The big difference is that this God invests all living creatures with 'fear and dread' of humans—a conclusion resulting in total domination. Or as a later text articulates in Deuteronomy 11:25:

> *No man shall be able to stand against you; the Lord your God will lay the fear of you and the dread of you upon all the Land that you shall tread, as he promised you.*

2. ***Colonise and Consume!***

Humans are now given the right to kill all living creatures except humans. God has transformed humans from herbivores into carnivores and thereby intensified their domination over all of nature.

3. ***The Blood Factor!***

Prior to this point, living creatures, including human beings, have been identified as ground or Land-made: made from *adamah* (ground) and identified as *nephesh chayyah* (living beings). Living beings are animated by the breath of life that comes directly from God. Now a new dimension is revealed; living beings have a sacred component called 'blood', which is the 'life' of the living being that comes from the Creator.

Human beings may be carnivores but they are not permitted to drink blood. The 'life' blood of the living being belongs to the colonial God; only the flesh is available for humans to consume. In the pre-colonial narrative of Genesis 2, humans are not identified as carnivores. Humans eat from the fruit of the trees of the bushland in Eden and live with the animals as members of their family (Chapter 3).

4. ***The image factor!***

While animals are free to kill animals, humans are not free to kill each other. The basis for this mandate is twofold: the killing involves spilling the life blood of another being made in the image of *Elohim* (gods or God); possessing the image of the *Elohim*, humans represent God or the gods by exercising power over all living creatures and the Land. To kill one such human being is to smash a divine image residing on the Land.

Whether the Hebrew *Elohim* is to be understood here as referring to God or the divine beings with whom God consults in Genesis 1:26 to make humans in 'our Image', is probably is of little significance. After the Flood, humans are clearly informed by this God that they possess an image of God/the gods that empowers them to dominate the Land and all Land beings.

The Voice of the First Nations

From our perspective, this blatant colonial tradition which confirms the original harsh mandate to dominate the Land and all living creatures of the Land (Gen 1:26–28), also reflects the colonial worldview and colonial actions of the Europeans peoples who invaded and colonised the Land of Australia. We, the First Nations of Australia, experienced a colonial oppression comparable to the colonial mandate reflected in this conclusion of the Flood narrative in the Bible (Gen 9:1–3).

Our response is to discern the falsity of this biblical tradition, recall the truths of our First Nations relationship with the Land and the Land Beings of our Country and to endorse the alternate *imago Terrae* retrieved in Chapter 2 of this volume.

As First Nations Christians, we are not only free to take this stand because of our rich spiritual relationship with the Land and the Creator Spirit in the Land; because we believe that the Christ we know has liberated us from the sin of colonial control and freed us to correct ancient biblical narratives and retrieve the underlying spirit of the Gospel that is colonial-free.

Chapter Eleven
The Rainbow Narrative: A Treaty with the Land and Land Beings

The third conclusion
to the biblical Flood narratives
relates to a treaty (a covenant)
that God
makes with the Land
and all the Land beings
to never again
send a life-destroying flood.

The rainbow is the sign rising up
from the Land to the sky
and back to the Land
to remind God,
of his treaty
with the Land.

The Colonial Free Narrative of Genesis 9:8–17

A Treaty with the Land Beings and the Land

God said to Noah and his family, 'Behold, I am now making my Treaty with you and with your descendants, and with all living beings who are with you: the birds, the animals and the beasts of the field, everything that came out of the ark with you.

I make my Treaty with you: never again will all flesh be cut off by the waters of a flood and never again will there be a flood to destroy the Land.'

Then God said, 'This is the sign of the Treaty I am making between me and you and every living creature who is with you, for all future generations: I will set a rainbow in the clouds and it will be a sign of the Treaty between me and the Land.

When I bring clouds over the Land, the rainbow will be seen in the clouds. And I will remember my Treaty which is between me and every living being of all flesh; and the waters will never again become a flood to destroy all flesh.

When the rainbow is in the clouds, I will look upon it and remember the eternal Treaty between God and every living being of all flesh that in on the Land.'

God said to Noah, 'This is the sign of the Treaty that I have made between me and all flesh on the Land'.

Analysis

The Third Conclusion

These verses represent a surprising third conclusion to the Flood narratives.

In the first conclusion, Noah builds an altar, and his God is delighted and promises to never again destroy every living being (Gen 8:20–22).

In the second conclusion, God blesses Noah and repeats the mandate to dominate recorded in the original *imago Dei* text, when he again submits all living beings into the hands of the humans (Gen 9:1–7).

In the third conclusion, God repeats the promise to never again send a flood and confirms his promise by making a treaty with all Land beings and the Land itself.

The significance of the third conclusion is that it overrides or supersedes the previous conclusions and introduces a positive new relationship between the Spirit of God, the Land and the Land beings.

The Term Berit

Perhaps it is helpful at the outset to explain our use of the term 'treaty' rather than 'covenant' used here to translate the Hebrew term *berit*. A covenant is understood to be an agreement between two parties. The covenant between God and the Israelites involves both parties: God makes Israel his people and they in turn are obliged to obey his commands (Exod 19:5).

In this Genesis 9 account, the *berit* is somewhat different.

- First, this *berit* is a unilateral promise of God to never again be violent and send another flood. There is no stated expectation or demand that Noah and his descendants need to play a designated role as respondents to a covenant agreement. This treaty is a free gift of the Creator Spirit.
- Second, this *berit* is not only a promise addressed to human beings, but is also addressed to all living beings and, in addition, to the Land itself. God's primal treaty is not with Israel, but with the Land and the primal Land beings.
- Third, this *berit* is accompanied by a 'sign' or 'witness', a feature that is frequently associated with treaties in the ancient Near East and First Nations Australia. The sign or witness is to be forever rising into the clouds to remind God of the Treaty that God has made with the Land and its Land beings.

The Spiritual Bond

If we recognise that this text represents a treaty with the Land, we can appreciate the spiritual bond that exists between the Creator Spirit and the Land. This is not the celestial Overlord who commissions humans to 'rule' of the living creatures and 'subdue' the Land (as in Gen 1:26–28). The Creator Spirit is here bonding with the Land and establishing a formal Treaty to testify to the Land's spiritual significance.

Just as significant is the character of this God who is constantly aware of the welfare of the Land and Land beings. This God will be reminded of the Treaty whenever a rainbow rises from the Land into the clouds and returns to the Land.

The Flood narrative also reminds us that the Land was once submerged by the waters as it was in the primal world of Genesis 1:1–2. God welcomed the Land when she appeared from beneath the primal waters (Gen 1:9–10). After the Flood, the Land again appears from the waters and is welcomed by God with a Treaty.

Covenants

It may be valuable to note, at this point, that the Treaty or Rainbow Covenant is the first of three main covenants/treaties God makes in the Hebrew Scriptures.

1. *The Rainbow Covenant* in which the Creator Spirit makes a treaty with the Land and promises to sustain the Land and all its living beings.
2. *The colonial-free Abraham covenant* in which El Shaddai, the Creator Spirit of Canaan, promises Abraham that through him many peoples will be blessed.
3. *The colonial Mosaic covenant* in which YHWH promises the Israelites that they will be able to colonise Canaan.

Identification

I am the rainbow
that rises from the Land
and reaches into the Sky.

When you see me rise
you know the Rainbow Spirit is rising,
declaring in bold colours:
'I will be true to my Treaty with Life
and with the Land to never
destroy the Land with a violent flood'.

So celebrate the Treaty
every time you see me rising
with the Rainbow Spirit
and returning to the Land.

Voice of the First Nations

The Voice of Wally Fejo

From my perspective, God, the Rainbow Spirit, is not outside the Land, but deep within her, so when the Land is overcome by the Flood, the Rainbow Spirit experiences a return to the Deep:

> *When the Earth/Land is concealed by water, the situation returns to the way it was in the beginning of the Dreaming (Gen 1.2). The Earth/Land is beneath the waters again. God is not at some distance watching the flood with an expression of justified anger. God experiences the Flood, the death of life on Earth/Land.*[1]

1. Wally Fejo, 'The Voice of Earth: An Indigenous Reading of Genesis 9', in *The Earth Story in Genesis*. Earth Bible 2, edited by Norman Habel & Shirley Wurst (Sheffield: Sheffield Academic Press, 2000), 142.

Whether we view the Creator Spirit as a force within the Flood waters or a 'spirit' hovering over the face of the waters (as in Gen 1:2), this tradition clearly portrays an intimate association of this God with the Land and the Land beings, an association that leads to a Treaty.

It also reflects on the relevance of the covenant/treaty God makes with the Land:

> *The covenant with all living creatures in Genesis 9 is the voice of God speaking from within the Earth/Land to Earth's creatures. The covenant reflects God's concern for the Earth/Land as a subject of permanent worth. The covenant honours all life, not just human life.*
>
> *God's covenant with all living things means that God relates to the animals, birds and other living creatures on Earth as living subjects, not simply as mindless objects. God makes the same personal promise to kangaroos and crocodiles, to turtles and beetles, as to human beings.*[2]

The Creator Spirit makes the same personal promise to the Land as a living entity—not as mindless matter. And the rainbow is a sign of that personal relationship.

> *The rainbow is a sign, a clear communication from God about God's relationship with Earth/Land, another expression of God's voice rising from the Earth/Land.*[3]
>
> *The rainbow in turn points to our responsibility to be partners with God, custodians of creation. That means reconnecting what is broken on Earth. The rainbow comes from the Earth/Land and returns to the Earth/Land as a symmetrical arc, reflecting all the delicate colours of the Earth/Land. The rainbow is also a reminder to us of the balance in creation that we are called to restore.*[4]

From the perspective of First Nations Australia, the rainbow ought to be a reminder to the colonists to restore the Land violated by nuclear explosions, Landscape clearing and, more recently, bushfires that destroy sacred sites.

---

2. Fejo, 'The Voice of Earth', 143.
3. Fejo, 'The Voice of Earth, 144.
4. Fejo, 'The Voice of Earth', 145.

The rainbow is not only a sign of healing, but also a sign of the Presence of the Creator Spirit that the colonists ought to also consider:

> *For many indigenous peoples in Australia, the rainbow is more than a meteorological phenomenon. The rainbow is a revelation of the Rainbow Spirit emerging from within the Earth/Land.*[5]

Or as Uncle George, one of the Rainbow Spirit elders, said to Uncle Norm: '*When I see the rainbow, as an Aborigine, all I know is God from eternity coming down here where I am*'.

5. Fejo, 'The Voice of Earth', 145.

Chapter Twelve
The Colonial Ham Tradition: Canaanites Cursed into Slavery

This narrative
preserves a blatantly colonial tradition
that provided a legendary basis
for Israelites who sought to take
possession
of the Land of Canaan
and view the Canaanites
as cursed peoples
whom God had authorised them
to destroy,
with their colonial God
leading the way.

A Colonial Tradition—Genesis 9:18–29

The Curse of the Canaanites

The sons of Noah who went forth from the ark were Shem, Ham and Japheth. Ham was the father of Canaan. These three were the sons of Noah and from these the whole Land was peopled.

Noah was the first tiller of the ground. He planted a vineyard; he drank wine and became drunk and lay naked in his tent. And Ham, the father of Canaan, saw the nakedness of his father, and told his two brothers outside. Then Shem and Japheth took a garment, laid it upon their shoulders, walked backward and covered the nakedness of their father. Their faces were turned away and they did not see their father's nakedness.

When Noah awoke from his wine and knew what his youngest son had done to him, he said

> *'Cursed be Canaan,*
> *a slave of slaves will he be to his brothers.'*
> *He also said,*
> *'Blessed by YHWH, my God, be Shem,*
> *and let Canaan be his slave.*
> *May God increase Japheth*
> *and let him dwell in the tents of Shem*
> *and let Canaan be his slave.'*

After the Flood Noah lived 350 years. All the days of Noah were 950 years and he died.

Analysis

The Approval of Slavery

This colonial narrative provides a brazen legendary tradition that views the Canaanites—the sons of Canaan—as cursed by their ancestor Noah. This tradition ignores the numerous colonial-free traditions found in Genesis 12–25 where Abraham and his household:

- settle peacefully in Canaan
- become allies with Canaanite communities (Gen 14:13)
- recognise El, the Creator Spirit of Canaan (Gen 14:19–20)
- make a formal treaty with a Canaanite family (Gen 21:22–32).

That Noah was less than blameless when he becomes drunk is ignored.

Canaan is cursed because his father Ham has seen Noah naked and did not hide the father's nakedness. Ham's mistake hardly justifies a lifetime of curse for his progeny.

For the colonial Israelites, however, the curse helps justify their dispossession of the so-called Promised Land of Canaan and a lifetime of slavery.

From a colonial perspective, this text announces a change in society: the divinely approved advent of colonial slavery.

The text may also reflect a popular mythology that the alleged sexual depravity of the Canaanites was also used to justify the Israelite invasion of Canaan (*cf* Lev 18).

The Focus on Ham

Mark Brett, however, discerns an alternative understanding of how the text has been edited and interpreted:

> *A close reading of these chapters (Gen 9–11) would suggest that the 'children of Ham' are those empire builders who are guilty of crimes of dominance. Colonisers would be the ones who stand under Noah's curse, not the indigenous peoples whose connection with the Land was swept aside.*[1]

In the language of our analysis, Brett seems to retrieve a 'de-colonised' version of this curse narrative, rescuing the peoples of Canaan from Noah's curse. Earlier, however, Brett states:

> *More significant for the Australian colonists was a widely spread conviction of their racial superiority, given sanction in mission history by an interpretation of the 'curse of Ham' in Gen 9.20–27 which saw the text as a universal curse on the black peoples that condemned them to slavery.*[2]

Clearly the time has come to de-colonise the curse on Canaan, by turning to the colonial-free traditions of the Abraham narratives. After all, 'all families of the Land shall bless themselves' through the blessing of Abraham (Gen 12:3). Abraham not only brings a blessing to the Canaanites, but also is blessed by El Elyon, the Creator Spirit of Canaan.

The Voice of the First Nations

At the First Nations workshop at Nunyara in March 2021, several of the First Nations Australia Christians confessed, in no uncertain terms, that not only were their parents and grandparents called sons of Ham—black and cursed—but that they too had been called 'black descendants of Ham'.

This colonial text needs to be denounced for what it is: 'the biblical basis for justifying slavery and for enabling so-called 'white' Christians to belittle and betray their First Nations brothers and sisters.

---

1. Mark Brett, *De-colonising God. The Bible in the Tides of Empire* (Sheffield: Sheffield Phoenix Press, 2008), 41.
2. Brett, *De-colonising God*, 10.

First Nations people suffered and endured great trauma at the hands of colonisers: they dehumanised our humanity; demonised our spirituality, culture and ceremonial practices, thereby designating First Nations peoples as the most inferior race on Earth.

Chapter Thirteen
The Tower of Babel
An Anti-*imago Dei* Tradition

The Tower of Babel Narrative
reflects an underlying critique of
the famous imago Dei tradition
found in Genesis 1:26–28.

Humans—
being in the image of God/the gods—
are not to assume
they have the imperial power to
reach the heavens
and be like the gods above;
they are expected
to represent diverse cultures
across the Land below.

A Colonial Free Tradition: Genesis 11:1–9

The Tower of Babel Narrative

The whole Land had one language and few words. As the people migrated from the East, they found a plain in the Land of Shinar and settled there.

And they said, 'Come on! Let us make bricks and bake them hard'. So they made bricks for building and bitumen for mortar.

Then they said, 'Come, let us build a city with a tower that reaches into the heavens, and let us make a name for ourselves, and not be scattered over the Land'.

Then God came down to see the city and the tower the sons of the Land beings had built.

Then God said, 'Behold they are one people and they all have one language. This is only the beginning of what they will do; and nothing they propose to do will be impossible for them. Come, let us go down and there confuse their language, that they may not understand one another's speech.'

So, God scattered them abroad from there over the face of the whole Land and they stopped building the city. Therefore, its name was called Babel because God confused the language of all the Land. From there God scattered them abroad over the face of all the Land.

Analysis

According to Mark Brett:

> *The whole point of the tower of Babel story is that this attempt to gain the high cultural ground, with a 'tower reaching up to the heavens' (Gen 11:4), is delusory and against God's intentions. No culture is represented as having divine favour, and when people are dispersed, they are shaped into a diversity languages and cultures.*[1]

In other words, human beings—who claimed to be made in the image of God/the gods—apparently decided to do more than 'rule the animal world' and 'control the Land'. They also had aspirations to reach into the heavens and make a name for themselves on high, aspirations that imply they are extending their role beyond the mandate to 'subdue the Land' (Gen 1:28). Their colonial dreams are too much for the gods above to tolerate—even though they are made in the image of God/the gods. Working together, humans had an enormous potential that enabled aspirations that the gods/God would not tolerate.

There is a sense that the 'mandate to dominate' is being exposed as false by a colonial-free Ancestral tradition that is alien to the colonial perspective of the original *imago Dei* text of Genesis 1:26–28

Like the critique of Genesis 6:1–4—where humans are made mortal—humans are here prevented from creating an empire that invades the skies, perhaps encroaches on the realm of the gods. In response, the primordial community is 'de-divinised' and dispersed to become a range of cultures—and no culture has the right to dominate another.

---

1. Brett, *De-colonising God*, 34.

The Voice of the First Nations

The Rainbow Spirit elders maintain:

> *Christian Aboriginal people point to the story of the Tower of Babel as further biblical support for our belief that the culture and Land of Australia are God-given. This story in Genesis ends with people being given languages and moving off in different directions as a result of God's intervention. Language is a bearer of culture; the Aboriginal languages are no less bearers of culture than the languages of other Lands.*[2]

---

2. Rainbow Spirit Elders, *Rainbow Spirit Theology*, 37.

Postscript Invitation

Our Postscript is an INVITATION.

Our Invitation is extended to:

- any First Nations people of Australia interested in exploring the colonial free traditions of the Bible
- First Nations Australians, who are Christians committed to sustaining their bond with the Land, and believe they are free to retrieve colonial-free narratives from the Bible that resonate with the truth they know from their pre-colonial heritage and culture
- Australians who are ready to de-colonise their minds and work with one or more of the First Nations people of Australia in exploring the colonial and colonial-free traditions of the Bible
- First Nations people and their colleagues from other countries who are willing to explore the colonial-free traditions of the Bible in the light of their colonial-free worldview.

Our Invitation includes:

- the possibility of writing a new volume in the *De-colonising the Biblical Narrative* series, focusing on a particular biblical book or streams of tradition within one book of the Bible or the Bible as a whole
- the option of writing an article or monograph exploring de-colonialising hermeneutics in a particular culture or biblical tradition,
- the challenge to create a ceremony in which a biblical Ancestral Narrative is told orally, and appropriate rites are performed to celebrate the colonial free tradition

- the option of preparing relevant artwork that highlights the colonial-free dimensions of a biblical Ancestral Narrative and publish the artwork along with a set of Ancestral Narratives.

Contact

If you or someone you know is ready to accept this Invitation—regardless of what option is being considered—please contact Auntie Anne (Anne Pattel-Gray) or Uncle Norm (Norman Habel):

- Anne Pattel-Gray (annepattelgray@gmail.com)
- Norman Habel (nhabel32@gmail.com)

The Challenge

This invitation is not a wild dream, but a challenge!

If you are willing to accept this invitation and retrieve a 'colonial-free' tradition from a biblical narrative, I swear by the Bible I will make sure it is printed and published.

Uncle Norm

Bibliography

Bell, Diane, *Daughter of the Dreaming* (Melbourne: McPhee Gribble, 1983).

Bird, Jimmy, 'The Bundaba Flood Story', in *Australian Aboriginal Flood Stories*, collected by W Douglas & Howard Coates, in *Creation,* 5, creation.com/australian-aboriginal-flood-stories.

Brett, Mark, 'Canto ergo sum: Indigenous Peoples and Postcolonial Theology', in *Pacifica,* 16 (2003): 247–56.

Brett, Mark, *De-colonising God. The Bible in the Tides of Empire* (Sheffield: Sheffield Phoenix Press, 2008).

Champion, Denise, *Anaditj* (Adelaide: Openbook Howden, 2021).

Charlesworth, Max, *Religion in Aboriginal Australia*, edited by Max Charlesworth (Brisbane: University of Queensland Press, 1984).

Davidson, Steed Vernyl, 'Lost Paradises: Tracing the Imperial Contours of Modern Tourism on Land and Peoples', in *People and Land: De-colonising Theologies*, edited by Jione Havea (Lanham: Lexington Books/Fortress Press, 2019), 15–34.

Edwards, WH, *Traditional Aboriginal Society* (Melbourne: Macmillan, 1987).

Fejo, Wally, 'The Voice of Earth: An Indigenous Reading of Genesis 9', in *The Earth Story in Genesis*. Earth Bible 2, edited by Norman Habel and Shirley Wurst (Sheffield: Sheffield Academic Press, 2000), 140–46.

Gilbert, Kevin, 'God at the Campfire and that Christ Fella' in *Aboriginal Spirituality: Past, Present, Future*, edited by Anne Pattel-Gray (Melbourne: HarperCollins, 1996), 54–65.

Habel, Norman, *Literary Criticism of the Old Testament* (Philadelphia: Fortress Press, 1971).

Habel, Norman, *The Land is Mine. Six Biblical Land Ideologies* (Minneapolis: Fortress Press, 1995).

Habel, Norman, *An Inconvenient Text* (Adelaide: ATF Press, 2009).

Habel, Norman, *The Birth, the Curse and the Greening of Earth* (Sheffield: Sheffield Phoenix Press, 2011).

Habel, Norman, *Acknowledgement of the Land and Faith of Aboriginal Custodians after Following the Abraham Trail* (Melbourne: Morning Star, 2018).

Habel, Norman & Peter Trudinger, *Exploring Ecological Hermeneutics* (Atlanta: Society of Biblical Literature, 2008).

Harrison, Peter (2005). '"Fill the Earth and Subdue It": Biblical Warrants for Colonisation in Seventeenth Century England', in *Journal of Biblical History*, 29/1 (2005): 3–23.

Havea, Jione, 'The Land Has Colours', in *People and Land: De-colonising Theologies*, edited by Jione Havea (Lanham: Lexington Books/Fortress Press, 2019), 1–14.

Heinrichs, Steve, *Unsettling the Word. Biblical Experiments in De-colonisation*, edited by Steve Heinrichs (Canada: Mennonite Church, 2018).

Lake, Meredith, *The Bible in Australia: A Cultural History* (Sydney: NewSouth Publishing, 2018).

Mowaljarlai, David & Malnic, Jutta, *Yorro Yorro. Aboriginal Creation and the Renewal of Nature* (Rochester, Vermont: Inner Traditions, 1993).

Pattel-Gray, Anne, *Through Aboriginal Eyes—The Cry from the Wilderness* (Geneva: WCC Publications, 1991).

Pattel-Gray, Anne, *Aboriginal Spirituality: Past, Present, Future* (Melbourne: HarperCollins, 1996).

Pope, Marvin, *El in the Ugaritic Texts* (Brill: Leiden, 1955).

Prior, Michael, *The Bible and Colonialism. A Moral Critique* (Sheffield: Sheffield Academic Press, 1997).

Rainbow Spirit Elders, *Rainbow Spirit Theology. Towards an Australian Aboriginal Theology* (Adelaide: ATF Press, 2007).

Rose, Deborah, *Dingo Makes Us Human. Life and Land in Australian Aboriginal Culture* (Cambridge: Cambridge University Press, 1992).

Rosendale, George, *Spirituality for Aboriginal Christians* (Casuarina: Nugalinga College, 1993).

Ruknundra, Lazare S, 'Postcolonial Theory as a Hermeneutical Tool for Biblical Reading' in *HTS Theological Studies*, 64 (2008): 1–9.

Stanner, WEH, 'On Aboriginal Religion', in *Oceania Monograph*, 11 (Sydney: University of Sydney, 1959).

Strehlow, TGH, *Aranda Traditions* (Melbourne: Melbourne University Press, 1947).

Wilken, John, 'The Biblical Promised Land and Australian Aboriginal Peoples' in *The Australian Catholic Record,* lxxiv (1997): 86–98.

Wolde, Ellen van (1998) 'Facing the Earth: Primeval History in a New Perspective' in *The World of Genesis: Persons, Places, Perspectives*, in JSOTSup, 257, edited by PR Davies and DJA Clines (Sheffield: Sheffield Academic Press,1998), 22–47.

Von Rad, Gerhard, *Genesis. A Commentary* (London: SCM Press, 1972).

Yunupingu, Galarrwuy (1996). 'Concepts of Land and Spirituality' in *Aboriginal Spirituality: Past, Present, Future*, edited by Anne Pattel-Gray (Victoria: HarperCollins), 4–10.

Printed in the USA
CPSIA information can be obtained
at www.ICGtesting.com
JSHW080817080224
56754JS00005B/176